KII

at
Universal Orlando
2019

An Unofficial Guide for Parents

MARY DESILVA

Recent Books by Mary deSilva:

Fantastic Eats and Where to Find Them at Universal Orlando 2019

Geek's Guide to the Wizarding World of Harry Potter at Universal Orlando, 2019 Edition

Universal Orlando Magic Tips 2019, Saving Time and Money at Universal Studios and Islands of Adventure

Escape from the Mousetrap 2016, Orlando Activities to Escape Walt Disney World

Escape from the Mousetrap 2015, Orlando Activities to Escape Walt Disney World

Geek's Guide to The Wizarding World of Harry Potter at Universal Orlando—A Guide for Wizards and Muggles

Universal Orlando Magic Tips 2016--Saving Time and Money at Universal Studios and Islands of Adventure

Universal Orlando Magic Tips 2015, Saving Time and Money at Universal Studios and Islands of Adventure

DEDICATION

For Patrick and Emily

ACKNOWLEDGEMENTS

Once again I have many to thank for helping me publish this book. I would like to than my travel writing guru, Barbara Twardowski, who has given me not only writing advice but also marketing advice. Thanks go to Susan and Heather O'Mahoney who accompany me on trips and are great photographers. Thanks to Danye Phillips for nutritional advice on dining at the parks. Thanks always to Kelly O'Mahoney, whose strength while battling brain cancer was an inspiration to me to pursue my dreams of travel writing. And thanks to my husband, Jim and children, Patrick and Emily for their support.

CONTENTS

INTRODUCTION

When it comes to Orlando travel, many assume that Walt Disney World is for kids and Universal Orlando is for adults. This view is taken because of the fairy tale and "princess" appeal of Disney and the contrasting adult themed events at Universal such as Halloween Horror Nights, fast roller coasters and the live concert series. Well, I'm here to tell you that Universal Orlando is loaded with appeal for kids! It has amazing attractions, shows, character dining, themed resorts and recreation options which are great for families with children of all ages!

If your little ones are fans of Dr. Seuss, the Simpsons, Sponge Bob, Harry Potter, Marvel Comics or the lovable Minions, Universal Orlando has hours and hours of the highest quality family entertainment waiting for you!

1 UNIVERSAL VERSUS DISNEY

When looking for a vacation with kids, the ideal situation is a place where there is entertainment for kids as well as adults. You can find this perfect situation at Universal Orlando. If you are looking for character meet and greet opportunities and attractions made specifically with kids in mind, you're at the right place. At these theme parks you'll find a princess, ogre, animals, witches, wizards, superheroes and even ghosts!

Many people just assume there is nothing for kids at Universal Orlando. I'm here to tell you that it is not true! Here is a comparison of some old favorites from Walt Disney World included characters, rides, parades and shows to similar and sometimes even better attractions at Universal. While these aren't perfect matches, they are good alternatives to Disney favorites. Although Universal Orlando only has two major theme parks at present plus one water park, you'll find there are several alternatives to your favorite Disney rides and characters.

Characters

Walt Disney World	Universal Studios	Islands of Adventure
Mickey and Minnie	The Minions, Margo, Edith and Agnes, Shrek and Donkey, The Simpsons, SpongeBob	Thing One and Thing Two
Cinderella, Snow White, Elsa	Princess Fiona (Shrek), Daphne & Velma (Scooby Doo), Betty Boop, Marilyn Monroe	The Ladies of Beauxbatons
Star Wars Characters	Shaggy, Scooby, Fred, Velma and Daphne, Doc Brown, Stilt Walking Pharaohs, The Blues Brothers	Spiderman, Captain America, Storm, Wolverine, Dr. Doom, Jean Grey
Captain Hook and Villains	Gru and Vector, Beetlejuice	Dr. Doom

Rides and Attractions

Disney Ride	Universal Orlando Ride
Space Mountain	Revenge of the Mummy (US)
Mad Tea Party	Storm Force Accelatron (IOA)
Prince Charming Regal Carousel	Caro-Seuss-el (IOA)
Dumbo, Magic Carpets of Aladdin	One Fish, Two Fish, Red Fish, Blue Fish (IOA) or Kang & Kodos' Twirl 'n Hurl (US)

Disney Ride	Universal Orlando Ride
It's Tough to be a Bug, Muppet Vision 3D	Shrek 4-D, Despicable Me Minion Mayhem, The Simpsons (US)
Peter Pan's Flight	ET Adventure (US)
Many Adventures of Winnie the Pooh	The Cat in the Hat (IOA)
Dinosaur	Skull Island, Jurassic Park River Adventure (IOA)
Rock 'n Roller Coaster	Hollywood Rip Ride Rockit Coaster (US), The Incredible Hulk Coaster (IOA)
Splash Mountain	Dudley Do-Right's Ripsaw Falls, Jurassic Park River Adventure (IOA)
Big Thunder Railroad, Slinky Dog Dash	Flight of the Hippogriff (IOA)
Seven Dwarves Mine Train	Harry Potter and the Escape from Gringotts (US)
Tower of Terror	Dr. Doom's Fear Fall (IOA)
Barnstormer	Woody Woodpecker's Nuthouse Coaster (US)
Buzz Lightyear's Space Rangers Spin	Men in Black Alien Attack (US)
Kali River Rapids	Popeye & Bluto's Bilge Rat Barges (IOA)
Star Tours	Amazing Adventures of Spider-Man (IOA), Transformers (US)
Avatar Flight of Passage	Harry Potter and the Forbidden Journey (IOA)
Turtle Talk with Crush	The Mystic Fountain (IOA), The Knight Bus (US)
Casey Jr Soak & Splash Station	Curios George Goes to Town, Fievel's Playground

Disney Ride	Universal Orlando Ride
People Mover	High in the Sky Seuss Trolly Train

Landmarks

Walt Disney World	Universal Orlando
Cinderella's Castle	Hogwarts Castle
Star Wars, Galaxy's Edge	The Wizarding World of Harry Potter (US & IOA), Marvel Super Hero Island (IOA)
Fantasy Land	Seuss Landing, Woody Woodpecker's Kidzone (IOA)
Toy Story Land	Toon Lagoon
Sunset Boulevard at Hollywood Studios	Hollywood and New York (US)
Tom Sawyer's Island, The Boneyard	Camp Jurassic, Jurassic Park Discovery Center (IOA)

Shows and Parades

Disney Shows/Parades	Universal Shows/Parades
Disney Festival of Fantasy Parade	Universal's Superstar Parade
Once Upon a Time, Fantasmic	Universal Orlando's Cinematic Celebration, Nighttime Lights at Hogwarts Castle
Spirit of Aloha Dinner Show	Wantilan Luau, Caribbean Carnaval Dinner Show, The Blue Man Group
Monsters Inc. Laugh Floor	Universal's Horror Make-Up Show

2 THE PROOF IS IN THE PLANNING

If you are bringing kids to Universal Orlando, you can have one of two experiences. You end up hot, sunburned, exhausted, frustrated, and basically the kids make their parents decide to leave early and declare that they are NEVER going to a theme park again. Or, you can have a fun, happy experience and the parents are already planning next year's trip! What is the difference between these two types of experiences? It is all of matter of doing your homework before arriving!

Here are a few simple tips for planning a trip to Universal Orlando where Kids Rule!

Planning Tips:

- Buy comfortable walking shoes for everyone at least one month in advance.
- Start a walking regimen and get in shape.
- Visit when the crowds are low.

- Stay onsite.
- Purchase tickets online.
- Read the Riders' Guide. Click here for the Rider's Safety Guide.
- Be strategic when souvenir shopping.
- Watch the films associated with rides.
- Create a touring plan with your kids.

Following these simple strategies will ensure a great trip. We will go into more detail about each one of these tips in future chapters.

Packing for your Trip

Packing for a trip to Universal Orlando has a caveat. When air travel is a part of your trip, packing can be a problem because of the extra baggage fees. If your luggage allowance is limited, pack light. Each hotel has washing machines or laundry service. You can also plan a stop at a Walmart, Target or grocery store near your resort. If you don't have a car, you can use a ride share such as Uber or LYFT.

Tip: Southwest Airlines always allows 2 free checked bags and a carry-on bag.

Tip: The nearest Walmart to Universal Orlando is 8990 Turkey Lake Rd, (407) 351-2229.

Packing Essentials

Whether traveling with infants, small children or teens, there are necessary items you should bring with you to the theme parks. Keep in mind that the theme park security will check bags more thoroughly than in previous years due to heightened security.

The number one item to bring for all ages is sunscreen! Because of the tropical climate in central Florida, the weather can be warm to downright hot and humid most of the year! For most people, this means wearing clothing with more exposed skin susceptible to the sun's damaging rays. A bad sunburn can stop a vacation in its tracks! Applying and re-applying sunscreen several times per day is a must to prevent damaging and painful sunburns. Note: The average theme park guest does not apply sunscreen often enough to prevent sunburn.

Another great item to pack is a Sharpie permanent marker. Use a permanent marker to write contact information on your children's arm or belly in case your child is lost. For more about lost children see Chapter 5: Important Information.

Tip: Order an engraved silicone bracelet! Follow this link to order a customized engraved bracelet with vital information about allergies and parents contact info.

When bringing small children, having a stroller will make life easier. There is an incredible amount of walking involved in a theme park vacation. While kids might seem like they have endless energy, a stroller is essential for giving tired little ones not only a break from walking but also a comfortable place to sit or nap.

It is easy to rent a stroller at Universal Orlando at the front of each park. However, I recommend bringing your own stroller for several reasons:

- Navigating airports is much easier with a stroller. The flight attendants can gate check it for you.

- There is a very long walk from the parking lot to the entrance of the themeparks. Once you are past theme park security, you still have to travel through CityWalk, which can be crowded at park closing time. If the little ones are exhausted at the end of the day, you will be carrying them!

- There are walking pathways from most onsite hotels. Walking to the parks instead of water taxis or shuttles saves having to wait in another line.

- There are often long lines for stroller rental. Who needs to wait in an extra line?

- Park strollers are not allowed on Hogwarts Express. This may not seam like a problem, but getting another stroller once you get to the next park is yet another possible wait time!

So what if it is inconvenient to bring a stroller on the airplane? There are several rental companies in Orlando who rent strollers and will deliver to you at your hotel. A quick Google search will reveal several rental companies.

Bringing a backpack is essential if you're spending a full day at the parks no matter your age. For the little ones, you can pack snacks, baby needs, extra clothes and small toys or books to occupy time while waiting in queue. For teens and adults, it is a good idea because all of the large roller coasters have metal detectors. You will not be allowed to take cell phones or even pocket change with you. There is only a limited amount of temporary free lockers and most are too small for a big backpack. There is a charge for large size temporary lockers. In this case, it is a good idea to pay the all day fee to put everything in a backpack and leave it in an all-day locker.

Packing List for Infants and Small Children:

Sunscreen
Necessary medications
Baby needs (diapers, wipes, formula, etc.)
Individually wrapped snacks
Permanent marker
Rain ponchos (bring extra large ones to cover your stroller)
Packing List for Teens and Adults
Sunscreen

Sunglasses
flip flop sandals, for the water rides
Rain ponchos
Cell phone charging banks or cords
Sandwich size zip-top bags (to keep cell phones dry)
Lanyard for your passes (these are also sold at souvenir shops in the parks)

What NOT to pack for the theme park:

Bulky camera equipment
selfie sticks
sodas
hard sided coolers
chocolate candy

Tip: Pack an empty backpack in your suitcase! This bag can be packed and repacked each day before heading out to the theme parks. At the end of the trip, pack it for traveling with all of your souvenirs!

3 ADMISSION TO THE PARKS

Whether staying one night or ten, the first step in planning a Universal Orlando trip with kids is to familiarize yourself with park ticket options. There are Single Park tickets, Park-to-Park tickets, multi-day tickets and annual passes. Vacation packages can also be purchased which include lodging and even meals. Review the following to choose an option that is right for you.

Tip: Children under 3 get in free! There is no admission fee for children under 3 years of age. Children's ticket pricing is for ages 3-9.

Tip: Buy tickets online to save a substantial amount off the gate price.

FYI: The Following are online prices. Expect to pay at least $20 more per ticket at the ticket booth at the parks. All prices listed here are subject to change at any time.

Types of Tickets

Tickets are available as One Day tickets or Multiple Day Tickets. When purchasing online, you may choose one of these options:

One Park Per Day tickets include access to either Universal Studios or Islands of Adventure for one day during park hours.

Riding the Hogwarts Express train ride in The Wizarding World of Harry Potter is not included in one park per day tickets.

Park to Park tickets (similar to Disney's Park Hopper) allows unlimited access to two parks— Islands of Adventure and Universal Studios for one day during park hours. This type of ticket is required to ride the Hogwarts Express train ride in The Wizarding World of Harry Potter.

Two-Park Tickets include the two main theme parks —Universal Studios and Islands of Adventure.

Three-Park Tickets include the addition of Volcano Bay Waterpark.

Value Pricing One Day Tickets

1-Park, One Park Per Day Ticket:
Adult $114, Child (ages 3-9): $109

2-Park, One Day Ticket:
Adult $169, Child (ages 3-9): $164

Regular Pricing One Day Ticket

1-Park, One Park Per Day Ticket:
Adult $122, Child (ages 3-9): $117

2-Park, One Day Ticket:
Adult $177, Child (ages 3-9): $172

Anytime Pricing One Day Ticket

1-Park, One Park Per Day Ticket:
Adult $129, Child: $124 (ages 3-9)

2-Park, One Day Ticket:
Adult $184, Child: $179

Ticket Combos

Combo tickets are available in two types. With multi-day tickets, you may choose between Two Park Ticket Combos and Three Park Ticket Combos. Two Park ticket combos include the two original parks, Universal Studios and Islands of Adventure. Three Park ticket combos include a day at Volcano Bay Water Park for an extra $55. Ticket combos are also available with the Park to Park option and the One Park Per Day option.

Two Park Tickets

2 Park Tickets include Admission to Universal Studios and/or Islands of Adventure.

2-Park, One Park Per Day Tickets

2 Day Admission: Adult $214.99, Child: $204.99
3 Day Admission: Adult $234.99, Child: $224.99
4 Day Admission: Adult $244.99, Child: $234.99
5 Day Admission: Adult $254.99, Child: $244.99

2-Park, Park to Park Admission

This type of ticket is available for one day or multiple days. The more days you buy, the more you save. Park to Park access is required to ride the Hogwarts Express train ride which travels between the two main parks.

2 Day Admission: Adult: $274.99, Child $264.99
3 Day Admission: Adult: $294.99, Child $284.99
4 Day Admission: Adult: $304.99, Child $299.99
5 Day Admission: Adult: $324.99, Child $314.99

Three Park Tickets

Three park tickets include admission to Volcano Bay Water Park.

3-Park, One Park Per Day Tickets:

3-Day Admission: Adult: $244.99, Child: $234.99
4-Day Admission: Adult: $309.99, Child: $299.99
5-Day Admission: Adult: $324.99, Child: $314.99

3-Park, Park to Park Tickets:

2-Day Admission: Adult: $274.99, Child: $264.99
3-Day Admission: Adult: $294.99, Child: $284.99
4-Day Admission: Adult: $374.99, Child: $364.99
5-Day Admission: Adult: $389.99, Child: $399.99

Tip: If you visit more than once a year, the best value is an annual pass. See the section below.

Ticket Delivery Options

There are five options to receive your tickets.

Free ticket delivery options:

Mobile Ticket. This option is delivery by e-mail and to your account's Wallet. This is a useful option because you won't lose your tickets. However, keep your cell phone charged or you will not have use of your tickets.

Print at Home. With this option you'll have your tickets in advance. I never use this option because your printed paper tickets are difficult to manage and can be easily damaged.

Will Call Kiosks are self service terminals which allow you to pick up your passes either the day before entering the parks early in the morning. You may also pick up Will Call tickets at onsite hotel concierge desks. These are credit card sized tickets. I like this option when using a lanyard to keep your ticket, express pass, credit card and I.D. together. Be sure to have your confirmation number from your purchase for pickup.

There are two more delivery options with charges:

Ship to Home Domestic: $14. P. O. Box not available, allow 5 business days for processing and delivery. These will be paper card tickets.

Ship to Home International: $19. Allow 10-13 business days for processing and delivery. These will be paper card tickets.

Call Guest Services for more information at (407) 224-4233.

Annual Passes

If you will be visiting Universal Orlando for more four days or more, instead of buying Park to Park tickets, you may want to purchase an annual pass. The seasonal pass is the same price as a 4 day Park to Park pass, although there are black out dates.

Seasonal Annual Pass

2 Park Seasonal Pass: $304.99
3 Park Seasonal Pass: $403.99

The seasonal pass has black out dates included and does not include admission to special events such as Mardi Gras and concerts.

2019 Seasonal Pass Blockout Dates:

Universal Studios Florida™

2019 Blockout Dates:

Jan. 1 - 3, 2019
Apr. 12 - 27, 2019
Jul. 1 - 31, 2019
Dec. 21 - 31, 2019
2019 Concert dates*: Feb. 9, 16, 17, 23, Mar. 2, 9, 10, 16, 17, 23, 24, 30, 31

2020 Blockout Dates:

Jan. 1 – 3, 2020
Apr. 3 – 18, 2020
Jul. 1 – 31, 2020
Dec. 19 – 31, 2020

*Seasonal Passholders are blocked out of Universal Studios Florida™ on all concert dates and will only receive access to Universal's Islands of Adventure™.

Universal's Islands of Adventure™

2019 Blockout Dates:

>Jan. 1 - 3, 2019
>Apr. 12 - 27, 2019
>Jul. 1 - 31, 2019
>Dec. 21 - 31, 2019

2020 Blockout Dates:

>Jan. 1 – 3, 2020
>Apr. 3 – 18, 2020
>Jul. 1 – 31, 2020
>Dec. 19 – 31, 2020

Universal's Volcano Bay™

2019 Blockout Dates:

>Apr. 12 – 27, 2019
>Jun. 14 – Aug. 18, 2019

2020 Blockout Dates:

>Apr. 3 – 18, 2020
>Jun. 12 – Aug. 16, 2020

Note: Volcano Bay™ blockout dates apply to 3-Park Passes only.

Annual Power Pass

Power Pass benefits include 50% off parking in addition to discounts at hotels, special event tickets and Blue Man Group tickets. If you drive to Universal often or more than four days, it may be worth it to buy a Preferred Pass instead. The Power Pass has almost the same blackout dates as the Seasonal Pass. If you are not going to use a car, save money with the Seasonal Pass.

2 Park Power Pass: $354.99
3 Park Power Pass: $463.99

Power Pass Blockout Dates:

Universal Studios Florida™

2019 Blockout Dates:

Jan. 1 - 3, 2019
Apr. 12 - 27, 2019
Dec. 21 - 31, 2019

2020 Blockout Dates:

Jan. 1 – 3, 2020
Apr. 3 – 18, 2020
Dec. 19 – 31, 2020

Universal's Islands of Adventure™

2019 Blockout Dates:

    Jan. 1 - 3, 2019
    Apr. 12 - 27, 2019
    Dec. 21 - 31, 2019

2020 Blockout Dates:

    Jan. 1 – 3, 2020
    Apr. 3 – 18, 2020
    Dec. 19 – 31, 2020

Universal's Volcano Bay™

2019 Blockout Dates:

    Jun. 14 – Aug.18, 2019, before 4 pm.

2020 Blockout Dates:

    Jun. 12 – Aug. 16, 2020, before 4 pm.

Annual Preferred Pass

The Preferred Pass is a good deal for guests who want to take advantage of the free parking benefit. If you take a car, this benefit will soon pay for itself after a few days.
Tip: Buy only one Preferred Pass! Only one member of your party needs this pass to get the parking benefit or other discounts. Save by

purchasing less expensive passes for the rest of your family.

2 Park Preferred Pass: $394.99
3 Park Preferred Pass: $503.99

There are no blockout dates at Universal Studios™ or at Universal's Island of Adventure™ for Preferred Annual Passholders. Preferred Passholders are blocked out on the following dates:

Universal's Volcano Bay™

2019 Blockout Dates:

   Jul. 1 – Aug. 18, 2019, before 4pm

2020 Blockout Dates:

   Jul. 1 – Aug. 16, 2020, before 4pm

Annual Premier Pass

   The Premier Pass is the highest priced pass because there are several advantages. The benefits associated with this level pay for the increase in price as long as you use them. This pass is great for Florida residents who will actually visit the parks several times a year. Only purchase this option if you will use the added benefits such as the Halloween Horror Nights ticket and discounts on dining. For many families, the best bet is for only one member to have this type of pass for the parking and discounts, and the rest of the family purchases a less expensive pass.

2 Park Premier Pass: $559.99
3 Park Premier Pass: $733.99

Exclusive Premier Pass Benefits:

- Universal Express after 4:00 pm

- Free Valet Parking (tipping is expected, excludes holidays and special events)

- Free self parking

- Early Park Admission to the Wizarding World of Harry Potter

- 15% off on multi-day theme park admission tickets purchased at the front gate (Up to 6 people per transaction per day; not valid on tickets including Wet 'n Wild® admission, or Universal Express™ passes, or tickets with Universal Express™)

- One (1) free Halloween Horror Nights ticket* (select nights)

- 15% off all restaurants (excluding food & beverage carts and alcoholic beverages)

- 15% off at Universal Orlando™ select merchandise stores and carts (restrictions apply on select merchandise)

- All club access to CityWalk™ for Passholders (excludes concerts and special events)

- Save up to 30%1 off room rates at each Premier and Preferred on-site hotel or save up to 25%1 off room rates at Universal's Cabana Bay Beach Resort

- One (1) free Halloween Horror Nights ticket* (select nights)

- 15% off at select restaurants (excluding food & beverage carts and alcoholic beverages)

- 15% off at Universal Orlando™ owned and operated merchandise stores and carts (restrictions apply on select merchandise)
- All club access to CityWalk™ for Passholders (excludes concerts and special events)

- Save up to 30% off room rates at onsite hotels

- Free admission to select special events such as Mardi Gras and Grinchmas™

4 ONSITE RESORTS

Choosing a place to stay is one of the most important decisions you will make in planning a vacation with kids at Universal Orlando. Universal has six onsite hotels with a brand new hotel opening in the summer of 2019 and another opening in 2020.

All of Universal's onsite hotels are uniquely themed and offer great amenities for families. Each resort is managed by Loews Hotels, a hotel chain known for comfort and luxury. When it comes to families, Loews' slogan is, "Loews Loves Kids" with special welcome packs for kids checking into their Orlando deluxe hotels. These resorts are a great choice for families because of the prime location and their fabulous array of amenities. Some of these resorts also offer services such as babysitting, laundry service and all offer great dining options and complimentary transportation to the themeparks.

Guests at the onsite resorts receive Early Park Admission which allows guests admission to the theme parks one hour before the posted opening time. All onsite hotels also have complimentary Wifi. And to help parents, get their day started, Starbucks are located at most onsite hotels!

At every onsite resort, there are several amenities and services offered. Each hotel has a concierge and ticket center where guests can pick up their tickets before heading to the front gates of the themeparks. Onsite hotels offer self parking or valet parking (there is a parking fee at onsite hotels of $12-25 per day for self parking).

At each hotel, there is a Universal Studios Store which carries not only t-shirts and souvenirs, but also sundries such as newspapers, diapers, first aid items, snacks and more.

A little known amenity at onsite hotels is "pool hopping." Guests at any onsite resorts are allowed to visit neighboring resort pools. Many hotels offer "Dive In Movies" at the pool where parents can relax with a cocktail while the kids splash around.

The Hotel Dining Shuttle service is also available in the evenings to take onsite guests to the neighboring onsite resort restaurants which saves time and parking fees.

If you have need of a crib or rollaway bed, most hotels will allow the addition of one rollaway bed in the room. Cribs are complimentary but there is a limited number so request this at the time of your reservation. Microwaves may also be available for a fee of about $15 per day.

Severe Weather

Universal understands that it cannot predict what Mother Nature intends. Although Orlando is many miles inland, hurricanes and other severe weather can impact your long awaited vacation. For this reason, Universal has enacted a Severe Weather "No Questions Asked" Cancellation Policy. In the event you are not able to travel to Orlando due to an active named storm impacting your travel, they will help you re-schedule your vacation or give you a complete refund with no questions asked.

The Resorts

All of Universal Orlando's onsite resorts are managed by Loews Hotels. This resort group has a program called "Loews Loves Kids" where each child is a VIK—very important kid! There are special dining menus and activities. The program also offers:

• Night lights for easy sleeping

• Child-proofing kits for families with kids under four

• Free WiFi throughout our properties for that all-important "tablet time"

• Pool toys and games at our resorts

• Loews Loves Kids activity book

• Rollaways and cribs can be requested for most room types

• Suites and connecting rooms so your whole clan can stay connected without stress

Resort Categories

There are four categories of onsite hotels at Universal Orlando.
Value: The least expensive option of onsite resorts is actually about a mile offsite. These themed no frills resorts will have excellent recreation amenities, food court, Early Park Admission and free shuttles to the theme parks.

Prime Value: These themed resorts offer comfortable family accommodations with quality amenities, food court and limited table service dining options, recreational activities, complimentary shuttles to the themeparks and Early Park Admission.

Preferred Resorts: Offers high quality accommodations with high quality dining options, amenities including water taxis to the themeparks and Early Park Admission.

Premier Resorts: Offers luxury accommodations, spectacular amenities, fine dining options, complimentary Universal Express for each guest in the room, water taxis to the themeparks and Early Park Admission.

Value Resorts $
Starts at $85

Universal's Endless Summer Resort - Surfside Inn & Suites

In July of 2019, the first hotel of Universal's newest value resort opens: Surfside Inn & Suites. This hotel will be jointly run by Universal and Loews Hotel Management. This is a value option family friendly resort with great pools and outdoor amenities and a fun surf vibe. This resort will have guest rooms with two queen beds and two bedroom suites that sleep six.   The outdoor recreation amenities will be shared by both hotels. This is the first off-site hotel with onsite benefits.   Guests receive Early Park Admission and complementary transportation to the theme parks.

A sister hotel, Dockside Inn and Suites, will open in May 2020. Both hotels will be part of Universal's Endless Summer Resort, a vibrant and sunny retreat.

Prime Value Resorts $$
Starts at $120

Universal's Aventura Hotel

The Aventura is a prime value hotel which is the first onsite hotel jointly run by Universal and Loews Hotel Management. What separates this hotel from other onsite properties is the modern style and tech savvy room amenities. Each guest room has a tablet which controls the room functions such as lights, temperature. It works as your television remote (which might be a problem for non-tech savvy guests). This hotel is a high rise glass structure with a smaller footprint than the other large resorts. It is close enough to walk to Volcano Bay or CityWalk and the theme parks on the landscaped walking paths. There is a cocktail bar at the pool and a food court in the lobby with wonderful and varied dining selections with kids' favorites like a burger station, pizza station and gelato (try the Stratiatelli gelato). There are also asian noodles, sushi and a roast station. Something parents will like is an open air rooftop restaurant and bar.

As far as amenities for kids, there is a hotel pool with lounge chairs, tables and limited shaded areas. There is a new Virtual Reality game room, located on the second floor next to the fitness center. Enjoy another one of the hotel's high-tech features while testing your skills at popular virtual reality arcade games like Fruit Ninja, Merry Snowballs or Space

Pirate Trainer. Universal is planning to continue to update with new games as time goes on.

Kids Suites

Aventura Hotel has "Kids Suites" with private spaces for parents and kids. The 575 square foot room sleeps five guests and features a special interior area for the kids that includes two twin beds. You can put the little ones to sleep securely while parents can enjoy some downtime in a separate area that offers a king bed and a couch that converts into a deluxe, foam bed. The suite has one bathroom with a tub/shower combo or just a shower.

Loews Cabana Bay Beach Resort

The Loews Cabana Bay Beach Resort is Universal's by far an annual passholder's favorite onsite resort. At this resort, Kids Rule! There is something at every turn to entertain the entire family. The resort has a nostalgic retro theme with the emphasis on recreation and guests love the sights and sounds of America in the 1960's. When you drive up, notice the classic cars at the entrance and the retro decor. The accommodations combine modern amenities with retro decor. Kids will love the character appearances on Fridays.

Kids Rule at Cabana Bay!

Keeping kids entertained is the name of the

game at Cabana Bay Beach Resort. The resort features loads of amenities including a bowling alley, arcade games, outdoor games, pools and family friendly dining options include a food court with a variety of options for even the pickiest of eaters.

Kids and, adults for that matter, will enjoy the Game-O-Rama arcade with all of the latest video game machines as well as some old classics. On the second floor of the hotel lobby, kids will love Galaxy Bowl, a10-lane bowling alley. If you get hungry, the Galaxy Bowl Diner, a table service restaurant, is located inside the bowling alley.

If it's characters, your kids want to see, Character Greetings are held on Fridays from 5pm-7pm. You can expect to see the Minions, the Simpsons or even Scooby and Shaggy.

The Pools

Spending time at the hotel pool is essential for keeping cool in the heat of central Florida. At Cabana Bay, there are two separate pool courtyards with giant swimming pools. The Lazy River Courtyard is home to a relaxing lazy river, fire pit, and a poolside restaurant, the Hideaway Bar and Grill, home of great poolside nacho! FYI, tubes are not free at Cabana Bay. They are available for purchase or rental, but if you bring your own, the pool staff will inflate them for you.

The Cabana Courtyard is where you will find cabana rentals for shade and privacy. The Cabana pool has a sandy zero entry "beach" and is the perfect place for guests with small children. Cabanas are equipped with television, telephone, refrigerator, fan, and lounge chairs. At the pool, kids will love the interactive water play area as well as the water slide.

Poolside, there are activities such as chess, billiards and other family friendly games such as hula hoop contests. To escape the heat, there are shaded picnic tables and The Atomic Tonic poolside bar. Poolside movies are shown in the evenings which is a great way for parents to relax while the kids play in the evenings after a long day of theme park touring.

The Rooms

Standard hotel rooms at Cabana Bay Beach Resort feature 2 comfortable queen beds and flat screen televisions There are Courtyard, Poolside or Tower rooms available. These rooms are available with interior or exterior corridors.

For a little extra room, choose a Family Suite. These larger rooms sleep six and offer a small kitchenette including a mini refrigerator and microwave. These suites have larger bathrooms to accommodate the needs of larger families. The suites have a bedroom with two queen size beds and a living room with a sofa bed and chair. A partition separates the two rooms for a little privacy.

For even more room, Cabana Bay offers two bedroom suites with a view of Volcano Bay. These spacious, 772 square foot rooms offer 2 full beds in one bedroom, 1 queen bed in another, and a full-size sectional pull-out sofa in the living room. Plus, these suites include 2 full bathrooms, a kitchenette with mini refrigerator and sink. The maximum occupancy is 8 guests. Book early because these rooms are limited and very popular. Sorry, there are no king-size beds at Cabana Bay. Click here for more information or to book a room. I prefer to book rooms through the LoewsHotels.com.

Just for Parents

Just because this resort is geared to families doesn't mean there aren't options for adults. Adults who want a break from family activities can relax with an adult beverage at The Swizzle Lounge (in the lobby), with the same type of iconic retro themes. Another place to relax with a cocktail is at The Atomic Tonic, the Cabana Courtyard poolside bar.

Other amenities include a chance to get fit at the complimentary Jack LaLanne Physical Fitness Studio. This studio, based on Jack LaLanne, the original fitness guru, features Life Fitness weight training and cardiovascular equipment. Take a little time to peruse Jack LaLanne's career in memorabilia. The studio is complimentary to all Loews onsite hotel guests.

Tip: Avoid the lines waiting for theme park shuttles in the early morning and closing time by taking the walking trail. It's about a 10 minute walk.

Preferred Resorts $$$
Starts at $168

Loews Sapphire Falls Resort

Loews Sapphire Falls Resort has almost everything you expect from a premier hotel, but with a moderate price tag. This Caribbean-inspired hotel is described "an island jewel in the heart of an unforgettable adventure." It also has a convention center which connects to Royal Pacific Resort next door. The resort is across the street from Cabana Bay Beach Resort and on the waterway with access to water taxis.

Kids Rule at Sapphire Falls!

The island theme of the resort welcomes kids and adults with a more casual, type of experience. The resort was designed with loads of options to keep kids busy and entertained. To start, characters such as the Minions or the Simpsons greet kids every morning in the lobby.

The Pool

The beautifully landscaped 16,000-square-foot

swimming pool is the largest pool of all of the onsite resorts. The area is flanked by cascading waterfalls. There are two sandy areas, a children's play area, hot tub, fire pit and water slide. As with the other hotels, there is a large selection of lounge chair seating and private cabanas for rental.

For a bit of fun after the kids dry off, they can visit the Calypso Game room to enjoy the latest high-tech arcade and video games or visit the games court poolside.

The lobby is no exception when it comes to the theme. The first thing guests see is the "ruins" of a stone turret as the lobby centerpiece of the lobby.

The Rooms

There are guest rooms and suites of this resort are mix of modern Caribbean design and luxurious furnishings. Guest room beds are made up with luxurious cotton 300 count bed linens. The rooms have 49 inch TV's with On Demand in-room movies and video check out. The rooms have iHome clocks and iPod docking stations, Cuisinart single coffee pod brewers and there is also a mini-refrigerator. The bathrooms have "barn" style sliding doors and have separate bath and vanity area.

Guests staying at this on-site hotel enjoy exclusive benefits available to all onsite guests at Universal Orlando® Resort including Early Park Admission and transportation to the theme parks—

shuttle buses or water taxis.
Kids' Suites

Like some of the other onsite hotels, this resort has Kids' Suites. Each Kids' Suite features a king bed and two twin beds in a secure separate bedroom. The two separate rooms are connecting and feature a single entrance to the adult room. The children's room opens only into the adult's room, and not into the hallway. This 529 square foot room allows plenty of space for the entire family. Five guests are maximum number of guests allowed per kids suite.

Standard Guest Rooms

Sapphire Falls features several types of accommodations. Standard guest rooms have one king with a pull out sofa or two queens in 321 square feet. Rooms have the standard or resort view, lagoon view or pool view. My favorite view is Lagoon view because you can usually see the spires of Hogwarts!

Roomier Suites

The King Suite is a little roomier than the standard king rooms with 595 square feet. It features the addition of a separate sitting area. The Sapphire Suite has spacious king bed in a large bedroom, a dining area, living room with wet bar and two baths combine to create your own private island. The Sapphire Suite sleeps up to 5 and offers more than 851 square feet of space. The Hospitality Suite is perfect for entertaining a large group or perhaps a family reunion. The 1,358 square foot suite has a separate dining area, living area, kitchenette, full bath and bedroom. For the ultimate experience, there is a Presidential Suite.

Just for Parents

When parents need a time out at Sapphire Falls, there are a few options. Of course, when lounging by the pool, there are private cabanas for rent.

If you decide you're hungry while at the pool, Drhum Club Kantine offers a Tapas-style menu with fresh seafood and tropical drinks. Take your cocktail to the adjoining fire-pit area to relax in the evenings. Another spot for evening libations is the Strong Water Tavern, a rum and ceviche bar with an outdoor patio overlooking the lagoon. The tavern opens at 4pm for dinner, with daily rum tastings.

For indoor or al fresco dining, the Amatista Cookhouse has an exhibition kitchen which prepares fresh Caribbean cuisine for breakfast, lunch or dinner. This restaurant is the most family friendly onsite with a breakfast buffet and kid friendly menu options.

If you need a workout while staying at Sapphire Falls, visit the complimentary Kalina Health & Fitness Center featuring cardiovascular equipment, mats, dumbbells, dry sauna, and locker facilities.

Guests can also jog or walk along the landscaped walkways which are a great way to get to the themeparks. If you want to play golf, call the concierge to arrange a tee time and complimentary transportation with the Universal Orlando Golf Program.

Premier Resorts $$$$
Starts at $252

Loews Royal Pacific Resort

One of the most beautiful and serene resorts in the Loews chain is the Royal Pacific Resort. This hotel offers luxury as well as family amenities. As you enter the lobby, you'll feel as if you've arrived at a serene Balinese destination. The resort offers a beach, lagoon style pool, a luau dinner show, evening torch lighting ceremony, fine dining and a character breakfast.

The Royal Pacific Resort, which can accommodate large conventions, offers a kids club and can provide in room babysitting. Character dining is held on Saturdays in the Tahitian Room with a large menu which will appeal to kids' picky palettes. Other dining options include a sushi lounge, The Orchid Court and Jakes American Grill. Your best bet for dining with kids is the Islands Dining Room which serves breakfast, lunch and dinner and has a Wok Experience on select nights.

When parents want to relax while the kids spend some time at the landscaped swimming pool, they can dine and enjoy beverages at Bula, a poolside restaurant.

Kids Rule at Royal Pacific!

It's no secret that parents love the Balinese theme and luxurious accommodations and dining options at the Royal Pacific Resort. However, there are amenities for kids including an arcade, playground equipment, and a lending closet with toys and board games. The Royal Pacific is also home to the only hotel character dining experience.

Character Dining

At the Royal Pacific Resort, you can dine with all your favorite characters! The Despicable Me Character Breakfast invites you to dine with Gru and his Minions, Shaggy and Scooby, the Simpsons and Shrek and Fiona at the Tahitian Room across from the pool every Saturday morning.

Another unique dining experience happens on Saturday nights. The Wantilan Luau, a weekly Hawaiian dinner show featuring an all-you-can-eat buffet of Polynesian specialties, live Hawaiian music and hula and fire dancing. To reserve, call (407) 503-DINE (3463) or reserve online.

The Rooms

Royal Pacific Resort has several levels of accommodations with the star of the show being the Jurassic Park Kids Suites. These are family suites with a luxurious king bed room with a sofa bed for the parents and an adjoining room for the kids. The suite is themed to the Jurassic Park movies with two twin size beds, and a flat screen television. For safety reasons, kids' rooms always exit through the parents room.

Other accommodations at Royal Pacific Resort include standard and water view rooms with either 2 queen beds or one king bed. Rooms have Keurig coffee makers and a minibar. Water view rooms look out at the lagoon pool or the waterway. Standard view rooms look out at lush landscaped areas.

For a little extra luxury and space, Hospitality Parlour Suites include a comfortable living room area with a sofabed, upholstered chairs, flat screen TV and a desk. These rooms connect to a standard or water view King room or 2 Queen beds room. The common area has a bathroom and dining room with a large table which can seat 8 guests. There is a mini kitchen with a refrigerator, microwave and sink.

The Club Level

A favorite of repeat customers to this resort is Club rooms. Club rooms have access to The Royal Club Lounge which includes personal concierge services, complimentary continental breakfast, evening beer and wine, hot and cold hot d'oeuvres and "something sweet" each night. Complimentary coffee, tea and soft drinks are available all day. The lounge is open daily between 7:00 am - 9:30 pm.

The Pool

At Royal Pacific, the pool is a star. The lush surrounding landscaping enhances the Balinese theme. The pool area features a small secluded sand beach with complimentary beach chairs. Organized pool activities keep kids entertained including hula hoop contests, pool basketball, arts and crafts and weekly "dive-in" movies poolside. The Bula Bar is a poolside bar and grill. There are two hot tubs, a beach volleyball court, and private cabanas for rent, complete with TV, refrigerator, ceiling fan, and water, soda and fruit. For reservations, call (407) 503-3235.

Just for Parents

When parents need a little time on their own, this resort has lots of options. Childcare services are listed below. If you want a cocktail, the best place is the Orchid Court Lounge where you can enjoy not only cocktails but a full Japanese sushi menu. At Jake's American Grill, enjoy the "bomber" theme with a beer menu and cocktails at the bar and American favorites in the dining room. Parents can get a work-out in while staying at the Royal Pacific in the well equipped fitness room or go jogging or take a leisurely stroll on the landscaped walking path.

Hard Rock Hotel

Music fans' minds will be blown by the rock and roll "vibe" at Hard Rock Hotel. The California mission style hotel is a veritable rock and roll museum with memorabilia at every turn. The resort has something for rock stars of all ages. The one of a kind artifacts are said to be worth well over a million dollars and you'll believe it when you see Elvis' jumpsuit, Elton Johns blinged out boots and more.

Kids Rule at the Hard Rock Hotel!

Of all the onsite resorts, the pool area at the Hard Rock Hotel is the most unique. Kids will love the giant winding, palm tree lined zero entry pool. Classic rock and roll music is not only piped through the outdoor speakers, creating a fun and exciting atmosphere, but can also be heard underwater through a fantastic underwater sound system! Kids can climb through a rock formation to splash down through a 260-foot twisting water slide. There are two hot tubs and a zero entry baby pool with an interactive fountain and play area for the little ones. Teens might enjoy a spontaneous beach volleyball game on the sand court. The pool as well as the sand beach is lined with relaxing lounge chairs and private cabanas are available to rent, including amenities such as TV, refrigerator and ceiling fans. Lifeguards are on duty during busy times and pool servers are available to bring you a cold drink (a great amenity on hot days). On select nights, "dive-in" movies are shown poolside. This is a great way to relax after a long day at the theme parks, while lounging at the pool while the kids splash around.

The pool isn't the only amenity geared towards kids. The Game Room, the hotel's arcade, is next to the pool and open daily with the latest video games.

Sweets for the Sweet

When kids have finished their dinner are need to cool down with a sweet snack, visit Emack & Bolio's for ice cream, sorbets and frozen yogurts. Their sweets have fun, eclectic flavors such as Bye Bye Miss American Mud Pie, Deep Purple Cow, and Jumping Jack Grasshopper Pie. Sandwiches, wings, and pizzas are available as well as Starbucks coffee, cappuccinos and lattes.

The Rooms

An easy way to live like a rock star is to stay at the Hard Rock Hotel. Each of the 650 guest rooms stylishly furnished rooms are decorated with rock 'n' roll artwork. The 375 square foot standard rooms have garden view or pool views and a 32 inch flat panel TV. The beds are made with luxurious cotton 300 thread count linens, iHome clock, iPod dock station, Keurig coffee makers, wireless internet, and a mini refrigerator for your convenience.

Deluxe king and queen rooms offer more square feet of space and an added seating area. King rooms can accommodate 3 guests and queen rooms can accommodate 5 guests (with the addition of a rollaway bed). One and two-bedroom King Suites are great if you're bringing your whole entourage. Book connecting queen rooms for large families.

Future Rock Stars Suites

Like the other premier hotels, the Hard Rock Hotel has a limited number of their version of kids' suites. These are two-room suites which offer more space for families. The suites are 800 square feet with a king bedroom for the parents and two twin beds in the kids' room. The kids' room decor appeals to kids inner rock star with their own stage, TV, and a table and chairs.

Rock Royalty Lounge

Upgrading your stay to a Club Level room will make you feel like you're hanging back stage at a concert! The Rock Royalty Lounge offers guests some great complimentary amenities like access to the private themed lounge on the seventh floor with two TV viewing areas, continental breakfast (7am-10am), evening hors d'oeuvres(5pm-7pm), soft drinks and coffee all day, evening sweets (8:30pm-9:30pm) evening turndown service, cotton signature robes, and personal concierge services, business center. Royal Royalty guests also receive discounts on cabana rentals. The lounge is open daily 7:00am-10:00pm.

Hospitality Parlor Suites

Because Rock stars have to entertain their entourage, the Hard Rock Hotel has Hospitality Parlor Suites that feature a living room with entertainment area, dining room table and kitchenette with bar and the band manager's enclosed office area. At 1,250 square feet, this space can accommodate any rocker's needs.

The Graceland Suite

If you're the King of Rock 'n' Roll, or just want to party like him, book the Graceland Suite. This impressive suite is 2,000 square feet of luxurious accommodations. It's located on the club level floor and has added features like a baby Grand Piano, glass encased fireplace, and whirlpool tub. The master bedroom has a king bed and an additional connecting bedroom is also available to rent with two queen beds.

Just for Parents

There are several places for parents to take a "time-out" at the Hard Rock. While their little rockers are splashing at the pool, The Beach Club poolside bar and grill is a great place to order lunch or a cool drink and relax. If you're in the mood for a workout, check out the Body Rock Fitness Center. It has all of the latest fitness equipment and weights as well as his-and-hers saunas and a steam room. Take a walk or jog around the resort on the beautifully landscaped walking path. Stop by the hotel's concierge desk upon your arrival and ask about the 1.5- or 3.8-mile loops.

In the evening, a favorite of locals and resort guests is the Velvet Bar located in the hotel lobby. This lounge is the place for music lovers and is home to "Velvet Sessions" with headlining artists who entertain periodically. The lounge offers a full bar featuring martinis and appetizers. The lounge opens to the veranda with outdoor seating.

If you want something more substantial than appetizers, The Palm Restaurant is famous for prime cuts of beef, lobster and American and Italian specialties.

Tip: The Hard Rock Hotel is the closest onsite resort to the entrance of the theme parks. Save time in the mornings and closing time by choosing the walking path instead of water taxis.

Loews Portofino Bay Resort

The jewel of the onsite resorts is a resort which transports guests to Portofino Italy. The Portofino Bay Resort caters to those seeking luxury and relaxation during their stay at Universal. Customer

Service is at a whole new level—simply send a text to Guest Services with any requests! The Loews Loves Kids programs are designed to make it fun—and easy—for families to travel with children and teens. The resort offers a multitude of amenities including three swimming pools, a bocce ball court, a full service spa, several restaurants and transportation to nearby attractions such as Wet 'n Wild and SeaWorld.

Kids Rule at the Portofino Bay Resort

Kids will never get bored while staying at the Portofino Bay Resort. There are multiple pools among the amenities and recreation available to guests. You might want to book a couple of extra days during your stay.

The Pools

At the Beach Pool, families will enjoy the Roman aqueduct-themed waterslide, sandy beach and children's pool. There are two hot tubs and three colorful beach cabanas. The private cabanas have ceiling fans, plasma TV, refrigerator with water, soda and a fruit bowl. These are a great idea for guests with very young children who might need to avoid the heat. On certain nights, Dive-in Movies are shown poolside.

The Villa Pool is a more quiet, more formal resort setting and offers private cabana rentals and upgraded lounge chairs. The Hillside Pool is for adults who want a little privacy. Contact the Concierge at 407-503-1200 for more information on cabana rentals.

Play Ball, Italian Style

Bocce Ball is one of the world's oldest lawn bowling games. Bocce is played with eight large balls of two colors and one small target ball called the "Jack," or "Pallino." Bocce ball courts are located near the Villa Pool.

The Rooms

There are several different room choices at the Portofino Bay Resort. Room categories range from standard guest rooms to elegant suites with special amenities.

Despicable Me Kids' Suites

Of all of the onsite resorts, the kids' suites at the Portofino are the most epic! Based on Gru's laboratory and house in the film, Despicable Me, these two room kids' suites are sure to give a chuckle to even the grumpiest of guests. When you enter the suite, you'll see a lovely king room decorated in soft, calming colors with elegant furnishings and luxurious bedding. But, step through the bomb shelter door and you are entering the world of the Minions! The two full size beds are inspired by the missile beds for Gru's daughters, Margo, Edith and Agnes, and the wall behind the bed is covered in Minions! The room has its own flat screen TV and desk. Parents need not worry about the kids' safety. The kids room exits only through the parents room and there is no lock on their door. There are 18 kids suites but as you can guess, they are extremely popular. Book your suite early!

Standard guest rooms come in two varieties. The 450 square foot 2 queen room or the king room has a garden view or bay view which overlooks the scenic harbor. The rooms feature marble accents and elegant furnishings from Italy. Deluxe King and 2 Queen Rooms are larger with a roomier bathroom with separate tub and shower and bathrobes.

Club Level Rooms

At the Portofino, you can upgrade to the Club Level and enjoy the amenities of the Club Lounge including complimentary continental breakfast, evening beer and wine and additional privileges including complimentary admission to the fitness center at Mandara Spa. Additional Portofino Club Lounge amenities include personal concierge services, complimentary coffee, tea, and soft drinks throughout the day, both morning and afternoon breaks, hot & cold hors d'oeuvres each evening and "something sweet" each night. The lounge is open every day from 7am -10pm.

Portofino Parlor Suites with Connecting Rooms

Parlor Suites start at 900-1350 square feet and provide a living room with a sleeper sofa which sleeps two, a plush arm chair and flat screen TV. There is a desk area for getting work done and a bathroom with a stand up shower. The bedroom features either a king bed or 2 queens. There are also 2 bedroom parlor suites for a larger family.

Villa Parlor Suites with Connecting Rooms

Villa Parlor Suites have 1,110 square feet with 620 square feet of living space that includes a sofa bed which can accommodate two guests, an armchair, and a flat screen TV. There is a bathroom in the common area with a stand up shower, a dining area for eight guests, and a small kitchenette. This suite connects to a deluxe room with a king bed and a large bathroom that includes a tub, a separate shower and double sinks. Villa Suites overlook the seaside harbor. There is a larger Villa Parlor Suite which consists of 1,600 square feet and two separate bedrooms, each with a private bathroom.

Hospitality Parlor Suite with Connecting Garden View Rooms

This suite consists of 1,370 square feet with a large living room and murphy bed that can accommodate two guests, a plush armchair, a flat screen TV, and desk area. In the common area there is a bathroom with a shower, a dining area, and a kitchenette. The connecting bedroom features two comfortable queen beds or a king, with a bathroom with a tub and shower. The suite overlooks the Villa Piazza area (formal garden area). There is also a two bedroom Hospitality Suite with 2 bedrooms and consists of 1,820 square feet.

Just for Parents

While the Portofino Bay Resort has many options for kids, parents can find lots of ways to relax and enjoy each other. The hotel's elegant European theme lends itself to feeling pampered. The hotel pools are one way to relax. Whether or not you rent a cabana, all you need do is alert an attendant to request a cocktail or order food from Splendido Bar & Grill, poolside. The Hillside Pool on the hotel's east side, is an adults-only retreat that offers a more serene environment.

While at the pool, you might decide that extra pampering is just what you're looking for. The Mandara Spa® is a full service spa which has separate mens and women's areas. The spa is located between the Beach and Villa pools and has a large menu of spa treatments including Hot Stone Massage, Frangipani Hair and Scalp Treatment, Elemis Pro-Collagen Quartz Lift Facial as well as other massages, wraps, makeup services and a manicure menu. Call (407) 503-1244 for appointments and more information.

If golf is more your speed for a getaway, you're in luck. While at present there is no official golf course on Universal property, there is a Golf Universal Orlando® program for onsite guests. The concierge can arrange tee times at one of the participating courses and arrange complimentary transportation. For more information, please contact the concierge at 407-503-1200.

In the evenings, adults have lots of options. The Harbor Piazza is a great place to enjoy live music with Musica Della Notte. The hotel also has several dining options for parents to enjoy. Check out for authentic Italian Mama Della's Ristorante or Bice Ristorante for a fine Italian dining experience. For a glass of wine and appetizers try The Thirsty Fish just off the harbor. For a more American feel with a little Italia mixed in, head over to Bar American. You can also hop on the hotel dining shuttle to visit any of the other onsite hotels for dinner or cocktails.

Childcare Services

Each of the three Premier Resorts have Resort Kids Camps where kids can enjoy fun and entertainment while the adults enjoy time to themselves. Kids age 4-14, will enjoy being entertained while parents take some time of their own. Activities include arts and crafts, stories, computers, video games, movies, and board games. Availability is based on demand, please call for details.

Campo Portofino—Loews Portofino Bay Hotel
Call (407)503-1200 for reservations and
information

Camp Lil' Rock — Hard Rock Hotel
Call (407) 503-2200 for reservations and
information

The Mariner's Club — Loews Royal Pacific Resort
Call (407) 503-3200 for reservations and
information

At each location you can drop off your children
for a night full of games, movies, arts and crafts,
snacks, and other activities. Our highly trained staff
will entertain the kids until you return to collect
them.

Activity Centers are open during select evening
hours and are available to children ages 4–14 (must
be toilet trained).

There is a fee (based on number of children and
hours spent in the center) and advance reservations
are recommended.

Your hotel concierge can help arrange area
babysitting services. Be sure to contact the hotel
before your visit to ask for details.

5 DINING WITH KIDS

Finding nourishing meals at Universal Orlando is an important decision. Whether you're in the themeparks, at onsite resorts, or at CityWalk, there are some great restaurants which kids will enjoy while hopefully enjoying a nutritious meal.

Tip: For a complete guide to dining at Universal, download my new foodie's guide, Fantastic Eats and Where to Find Them at Universal Orlando.

Here are my picks for best kids dining by category:

Best Pizza: Red Oven Pizza, CityWalk or Sal's

Market Deli, Portofino Bay Resort

Best Burgers: Cowfish, CityWalk or NBC Grill & Brew

Best Ice Cream: Florean Fortesque's Ice Cream Parlour, Diagon Alley, Universal Studios

Best Nachos: Jimmy Buffet's Margaritaville, CityWalk

Best Themed Restaurant: Mythos, The Lost Continent, Islands of Adventure or Monsters Cafe, Universal Studios or The Three Broomsticks, Hogsmeade

Best Breakfast Buffet: The Kitchen, Loews Hard Rock Hotel

Character Dining

Disney hasn't cornered the market on character dining in Orlando. Universal Orlando is the only place where diners get to visit with the characters of Despicable Me including Gru and the Minions but also Spider-Man and Captain America.

At Universal Orlando, there are two current year round character dining experiences. The Despicable Me Character Breakfast and the Marvel Super Hero Dinner.

Marvel Character Dinner

The newest Character Dining Experience takes place at Islands of Adventure! Feast with your favorite heroes at the Marvel Character Dinner. It happens at Cafe 4 across from the Incredible Hulk Coaster in Marvel Super Hero Island. The characters you can expect to see are SpiderMan, Rogue, Storm, Wolverine, and Captain America. Diners will have their choice of an Italian buffet with assorted pizza, salads, pastas and desserts. The dining experience is held Thursdays through Sundays, beginning at 5:00 pm. Reservations are recommended.

Adults (Ages 10 and up) $49.99
Children (Ages 3-9) $24.99

Despicable Me Character Breakfast

Character dining is at its finest with the lovable Minions of Despicable Me. Guests will dine from a varied breakfast buffet with all of your favorites and you'll get to me Gru, Agnes, Margo, Edith and other Despicable Me characters. This dining experience is every Saturday with seating times at 8:00am, 9:30am and 11:00am. The price is $34.99 for adults and $20.99 for children ages 3-9. Reservations are highly recommended.

Seasonal Character Dining

There are two seasonal character dining

opportunities. The first is the Scareactors Dining Experience which is part of Halloween Horror Nights. This is a special event which required a separate ticket to the event and a ticket to the dinner. Halloween Horror Nights has a PG-13 rating which means the event is not appropriate for small children. However, teens love it! At the Scareactors dinner which is held at Monsters Cafe in Universal Studios, fiends from Universal classic horror movies visit your table. Expect to see the Mummy, Frankenstein and Dracula.

The Grinch and Friends Character Breakfast

During the very popular Grinchmas Celebration, you must not miss the chance to dine with the Grinch and friends! The Grinch & Friends Character Breakfast is held at Circus McGurkus Cafe Stoo-pendous at Universal's Islands of Adventure. Adult price $34.99+tax Child price (9 and under) $18.99+tax

*Reservations are required. After reserving and purchasing your dining experiences online, you must call 407-224-FOOD (3663) (EST 7:30am - 10pm Monday-Saturday; 7:30am - 9pm Sun) up to 24 hours before arriving to confirm your table.

**Admission to Islands of Adventure is not included.

Best Onsite Resort Dining for Kids

Whether or not you are staying onsite, there are dining opportunities from casual to elegant at the beautifully themed onsite resorts. Here are some of the best for kids.

Dining at Cabana Bay Beach Resort

Bayliner Diner—Food Court

Having a variety is always a good idea when traveling with kids. This food court is a quick and easy stop for any mealtime. At the Deli Station you can enjoy a deli sandwich on fresh baked bread along with a variety of bakery items. The International Station carries meal choices from around the world. The Pizza Station and Burger Station are always popular with kids and the Salad Station offers a healthy choice. Of course, kids love the Dessert Station featuring soft serve frozen yogurt cups with a choice of toppings, ICEE treats, bulk candy and more. The "Grab and Go" is great when you want snacks for the pool or to take with you on your way out.

Galaxy Bowl Restaurant

The Galaxy Bowl Restaurant is located in the bowling alley located on the 2nd floor of the hotel's lobby building. The restaurant features casual, table service dining amid the fun and energy of music and bowling.

The Hideaway Bar & Grille

There's no need to dry off while at the pool to satisfy hunger pangs. The poolside bar and grill offers specialty cocktails, beers, snacks, sandwiches and grilled items for lunch and dinner.

Loews Royal Pacific Resort Dining

Wantilan Luau

The themeparks aren't the only place for great entertainment. Visit Loews Royal Pacific Resort for an evening of authentic Polynesian food and entertainment at the Wantilan Luau, a weekly Hawaiian dinner show featuring an all-you-can-eat buffet of Polynesian specialties, live Hawaiian music and traditional hula dancing. The excitement of the hula and fire dancing increases when guests are enticed to join in the fun! Click here for the luau menu and info. Call 407-503-DINE (3463) or reserve online. Registration begins at 5:30 pm. Seating begins at 6:00 pm.

Islands Dining Room

If you cant make it to the Luau, you can still enjoy a Hula Dancer and Ukulele Player on Friday evenings at the Islands Dining Room. This restaurant is open for breakfast, lunch and dinner. On select days, The Wok Experience is available and is a Hibachi style dining experience. It has a special dining room just for kids, with kid-size tables and chairs, a flat-screen TV playing cartoons, a Bali-style play area and toys. A kids' menu is also available.

Bula Bar & Grill

Experience a Fiji welcome at Bula, the poolside bar and grill. This tropical spot has fruity drinks, sandwiches, and a Big Bula Burger.

Hard Rock Hotel Dining

The Kitchen has the best breakfast buffet by far at Universal Orlando. The restaurant is open for breakfast, lunch and dinner. Kids can hang out in the Kids' Crib which is decorated with CDs, colorful drumsticks, bean bag chairs and kid sized tables; and a big-screen TV to watch cartoons.

The Kitchen

At the Kitchen, you will not only find the best breakfast buffet with items like Bananas Foster Pancakes, but you will also find great burgers and the desserts are next level—out of this world!

Emack & Bolio's Marketplace

Emack & Bolio's is a Boston tradition and serves ice cream, sorbets and frozen yogurts. This quick service ice cream parlor offers eclectic flavors such as Deep Purple Cow. Pizza and wings are available here and coffee drinkers can enjoy an authentic

Starbucks latte, cappuccino or Frappuccino®. Candy, snacks and drinks are also available in the Marketplace.

Loews Portofino Bay Resort Dining

Trattoria del Porto

Experience a little Italia! The casual feeling of this restaurant is great for families or anyone wanting to relax at the indoor or outdoor tables. The restaurant is open daily for breakfast, lunch and dinner. The dinner menu features a special experience, Pasta Cuccina, which kids love. On certain nights, you can choose your own ingredients, type of pasta, and sauce while a chef cooks it all in front of you. The restaurant also features a children's play area with a child-size table and chairs, beanbags and a large-screen TV. A children's menu is also available.

Sal's Market Deli

Sal's is a great little market with a great assortment of Italian meats, cheeses, antipasto and salads, along with great pizzas, snacks and fresh fruit. Open daily from 11am–11pm.

Universal's Aventura Hotel Dining

Urban Pantry—Food Court

Urban Pantry is the food court in the lobby of Aventura. There are several stations for dining with made to order food which elevates the quality of what you order. The stations are: Burger, Pizza, Roast, Gelato and Noodle and Sushi. The gelato flavors here are divine. Try the Pistachio Nutella or the Straciatella.

Best CityWalk Dining for Kids

Whether you are taking a lunch break or winding down from a long day of touring the theme parks, a good meal may be just what you need. Universal CityWalk has a wide variety of restaurants from quick service to fine dining. There is quite a variety of choices from fresh sandwiches to hand-rolled sushi made to order to wood fired pizza and more.

Here is my list of the best CityWalk restaurants which will appeal to kids.

Bubba Gump Shrimp Company

Bubba Gump's is probably the best restaurant for kids at CityWalk. Kids can choose their main dish and sides from the kids menu as well as choose from the Kids Live Well menu from the National Restaurant Association which meets specific nutritional guidelines. The staff will delight your family with southern charm and kids enjoy trying on plaster casts of Forrest's running shoes and taking pictures with the Shrimp mascot. There are lots of great souvenirs to be found in the market after your meal. A gluten free menu is also available. Click here for the gluten free menu.

Toothsome Chocolate Emporium and Savory Feast Kitchen

Toothsome has quickly risen to the favorite position at CityWalk, mostly because of the incredible milkshakes. This is a full service restaurant with great burgers and appetizers. Inside the waiting area is a steampunk styled gift shop with a candy counter and made to order milkshake counter. There are two characters who roam the restaurant and greet guests—Dr. Penelope and her robot friend, Jacques.

Antojitos

Antojitos is not your average Mexican restaurant experience. Fresh ingredients are marinated, roasted or grilled to delicious perfection. The menu is based on Mexican street food. Aside from the delicious menu, kids will love the live mariachi band which performs nightly. Not only do they play traditional mariachi music, but the put their own spin on pop music favorites.

The Cowfish.Sushi.Burger.Bar

The Cowfish has something for everyone. As you walk in, kids can create their own fish on the interactive digital aquariums. The unique restaurant concept combines the ultimate burgers paired with awesome sushi. It sounds crazy but it has become the favorite eatery of CityWalk. There is a fantastic kids menu with mini burgers and peanut butter and jelly rolls "sushi" rolls. Ask for an outside table overlooking all the fun happening at CityWalk.

Jimmy Buffet's Margaritaville

This might seem like a place for adults to enjoy margaritas, and it is. But there is also a great array of menu items which will appeal to kids. There are also fun elements like an erupting Volcano!

Red Oven Pizza Bakery

Parents and kids will love the artisan pizzas made fresh while you wait. This is a quick service restaurant so the atmosphere is more relaxed. Try a white, red or my favorite, prosciutto and arugula pizza.

Sweets for the Sweet

As I've already mentioned, Toothsome Chocolate Emporium has the most fantastic sweet treats. The most popular items on the menu are the over the top shakes with flavors like, red velvet, key lime, s'mores and more. There are, however, great sundaes and other yummy sweet treats.

Voodoo Doughnut

The best doughnuts you'll ever try are at Voodoo Doughnut. There is a big variety with of cake, gluten free, vegan, and raised doughnuts. Try one of the original flavors like Memphis Mafia, Grape Ape, Maple Bacon Bar and Raspberry Romeo.

Menchie's Frozen Yogurt

When the Florida heat is at its highest, Menchies will help you cool off with this popular frozen yogurt. It's a good place for a quick treat.

Cold Stone Creamery

Cold Stone Creamery has been many people's favorite ice cream for 25 years, serving the freshest ice cream because of their signature process of preparing your custom ice cream creations on a frozen granite stone.

Cinnabon®

The perfect quick breakfast treat in the morning before heading into the theme parks is a hot out-of-the-oven luscious cinnamon roll. The good news is that it is open all day. Choose from the Pecanbons, Minibons, Seattle's Best Coffee, and soft serve ice cream.

Theme Park Dining

All around the themeparks you can find quick service carts where you can buy your average park fare: churros, popcorn, hot dogs, etc. However, Universal offers healthy snack options featuring whole fruits such as oranges and apples, fruit cups and more.

If you want a more special dining experience, the following are some great dining venues listed by their location in the parks with great themes and some nutritious dining options. Most sit down restaurants at Universal Orlando now offer vegetarian and plant based options.

Dining At Universal Studios

Production Central Dining

Monsters Cafe

Lovers of the classic horror movies will love the abundance of movie props and statues of Frankenstein, The Wolfman, and more. The menu has traditional park fare such as pizza, burgers, salads, and and rotisserie chicken.
Service Type: Quick Service, Lunch and Dinner $7-15

Hollywood Dining

Mel's Drive In

You'll think you've gone back in time to the 1950's at Mel's with their classic cars outside and authentic jukebox inside. Enjoy Burgers and Fries, Chicken Sandwiches, Chicken Fingers, Onion Rings, Root Beer Floats and Milk Shakes.
Hours: Lunch and Dinner Daily
Service Type: Quick Service

Tip: Mel's Drive In is the best place to view the start and end of Universal's Superstar Parade and see characters.

New York Dining

Louie's Italian Restaurant

You might recognize this restaurant's facade from the movie, The Godfather. Louie's, serves good Bronx's style pizza plus spaghetti & meatballs, fettuccini, Subs, Caesar Salad, Gelato and a plant based pasta option.
Hours: Lunch and Dinner daily
Service Type: Quick Service

Ben & Jerry's

Enjoy everyone's favorite ice cream, Ben & Jerry's, in Waffle Cones, Sundaes and Shakes, plus delicious Smoothies.

Hours: 11:00am to Park Close daily
Service Type: Quick Service

San Francisco Dining

Richter's Burger Co.

Grab a double cheeseburger or chicken sandwich, and fix it up with the fresh fixings bar. There are also grilled chicken salads, an Impossible burger and milk shakes.
Hours: Lunch and Dinner daily
Service Type: Quick Service

Diagon Alley Dining:

Leaky Cauldron™

Harry Potter fans need go no further to satisfy their hunger than the Leaky Cauldron. Dine on traditional British specialties and sip some specially concocted wizard friendly drinks or try the famous Butterbeer! Menu items include Toad in the Hole, Cottage Pie, fish and chips, and Bangers & Mash. The children's menu offers the basics, such as macaroni and cheese and chicken fingers. Of course the menu also offers Butterbeer, both original and frozen as well as a dessert—Butterbeer Potted Cream.
Service Type: Pub Style Quick Service
Hours: Breakfast, Lunch and Dinner daily

Florean Fortescue's Ice-Cream Parlour

Butterbeer soft serve ice cream and Harry Potter's favorite, hard packed Strawberry Peanutbutter ice cream plus many more flavors can be found in either scoop or soft serve ice creams. Try the chocolate raspberry, Harry's first "taste" in the wizarding world.
Service Type: Quick Service
Hours: From park open to one hour before park closing

Springfield Dining—Fast Food Boulevard

All of Homer's favorites at Fast Food Boulevard are listed below. These are definitely not the finest eateries at the parks, but there are some quite tasty eats here. My personal favorite—the Basket O' Calamari at the Frying Dutchman.
Hours: 11am - 1 hour prior to park close
Service Type: Quick Service

Krusty Burger

This spot has a satiric spin on standard theme park favorites. Krusty the Clown's faves: Krusty Burger, Clogger Burger, The Ribwich, Sideshow Bob Foot Long, or a Heat Lamp Dog.

The Frying Dutchman

Find all of the Dutchman's seafood specialities here. Try the Basket O' Shrimp, the Basket O'

Calamari, the Battered and Plattered Fish, or the Clam Chowd-arr.

Cletus' Chicken Shack

While not originally part of the Simpson's show, this spot has one favorite of repeat park guests—the Chicken & Waffle Sandwich. Also try the Double Batter Chicken Platter, Chicken Arms (tenders) and Chicken Thumbs (wings) with Buffalo or BBQ sauce.

Luigi's Pizza

It may be Springfield's finest Italian eatery but personally, I'd rather go back to Louie's. Choose from the Cheese Pizza, the Vegetarian Pizza, or the Meat Liker's Pizza.

Lisa's Teahouse of Horror

Oh the horror! Healthy pre-packaged salads, veggie sandwiches, turkey wraps, hummus, fruit plates, fruit cups, and assorted yogurts are all available here.

Lard Lad Donuts

This is the place which "towers" above all other D'oh-nuts! Two or more can split the local favorite, The Big Pink iced donut or the D'Oh-Nut Sundae.
Hours: 9am - park close
Service Type: Quick Service

Bumblebee Man's Taco Truck

Get your Mexican street food—Springfield style at Bumblebee Man's Taco Truck. There are surprisingly good and healthy tacos including the Korean Beef Taco, Carne Asada Tacos and Chicken Tacos.
Hours: 11am - close, time varies
Service Type: Quick Service

Moe's Tavern

At Moe's, try a real Duff Beer, locally brewed exclusively for Universal Orlando® Resort. A Flaming Moe, non-alcoholic, will also wet your whistle with its "smoke" effect! Be sure to try the Love Tester machine in the corner. If you just want to enjoy the atmosphere, ask to be seated here when you enter Fast Food Boulevard.
Hours: closes 1 hour prior to park close

Woody Woodpeckers KidZone Dining

Kid Zone Pizza Company

Your kids will be spending lots of time playing at the KidZone® so it is great that you can zip into Kid Zone Pizza Company for any of the kids' favorites on their menu—pizza and chicken fingers, salads and fruit cups.
Hours:Lunch and Dinner daily
Service Type: Quick Service

Islands of Adventure Dining

Port of Entry Dining:

Confisco Grill

Confisco Grill is decorated with artifacts collected by world travels and some extinct attractions. You'll find an array of dishes from around the world including Grilled Sandwiches and Burgers, Soup, Salads, Fajitas, Pasta, and a Full Bar. This is Islands of Adventure's character dining venue.
Service Type: Full Service, Lunch and Dinner Daily
$10 to $18

Seuss Landing Dining

At Seuss Landing, you've reached a kid's paradise of dining establishments!

Circus McGurkus Cafe Stoo-Pendous

Young kids could not find a more fun and entertaining eatery under the big top of a circus tent where Seuss creatures perform overhead. The High in the Sky Trolley Chain passes through the from time to time. The kid-friendly menu features Fried Chicken, Spaghetti, Pizza, Cheeseburgers and Chicken Caesar Salad.
Service Type: Quick Service, Lunch and Dinner

Green Eggs and Ham Cafe (open seasonally)

Yes, that's right!   This is the place to try the world's most colorful eggs! Try the tasty Green Eggs and Ham Sandwiches or Chicken Fingers, Hamburgers and Cheeseburgers!
Only open seasonally (during peak crowd times like Summer)
Service Type: Quick Service
Price Range: From $6 to $8

Hop on Pop Ice Cream Shop

Florida is hot, but ice cream is not! Don't miss the Sundae on a Stick, Waffle Cones, Dippin' Dots and Root Beer Floats.
Open seasonally please check park map
Service Type: Quick Service
Price Range: From $3 to $5

Honk Honkers

At this little candy shop, you can get cotton candy twice the size of your head! You can also get Unicorn Cotton Candy with crunchy candle mix-ins.

Lost Continent Dining

Mythos Restaurant

While not for everyone, if you are looking to elevate your theme park dining experience, then Mythos is the place to try. Being named the world's

"Best Theme Park Restaurant" six years in a row is a pretty impressive achievement. Mythos has one of the most impressive facades in the park. A towering rock formation with a cascading waterfall from a "wizard's" mouth and other mythic creatures welcome guests to The Lost Continent. The interior decor is just as amazing with mystical rock carvings. There is outdoor seating offering a spectacular view of the lake and the rest of the park.

The menu does not remotely resemble anything offered in either park. The menu has Mediterranean appetizers, tempting salads and entrees, but also offers burgers and wraps for the pickier eater. Kids will love the surroundings and want to explore each nook and cranny. Vegan and gluten free dishes are available here and there is also a separate children's menu.
Hours: Lunch daily
Reservations accepted: 407-224-FOOD (3663).

Fire Eaters Grill

While kids inner explorers are developing in The Lost Continent, they'll love what's offered at Fire Eaters Grill. This popular spot has something every kid will like on its menu such as Sindbad's Grilled Gyros, Fiery Chicken Stingers, Chicken Fingers, Hot Dogs and Salads.
Service Type: Quick Service, 11:00am to Park Close daily
From $6 to $8

Hogsmeade Dining

The Three Broomsticks

Sitting in this wizarding world quick-service restaurant is like you are a part of the film, Harry Potter and the Prisoner of Azkaban! The restaurant was actually completed before the film so the accuracy is great. The menu features British fare and American favorites. If traveling with a large family, try the Great Feast which has rotisserie chicken, ribs, corn on the cob, veggies, and roasted potatoes.
Service Type: Quick Service
From $6-$15

Jurassic Park Dining

Jurassic Park is one of the best areas for kids in either park, so plan on spending time here. There are several dining options here which will satisfy kids' picky palettes.

Pizza Predattoria

When you have a T-Rex sized appetite, you can satisfy it here with Fresh Baked Pizzas, Meatball Subs, Chicken Caesar Salads and more.
Service Type: Quick Service, Lunch and Dinner daily

The Burger Digs

The Burger Digs is attached to the Jurassic Park

Discovery Center. The menu includes your basic Burgers and Garden Burgers, Chicken Sandwiches, and Chicken Tenders but also features a fixings bar to add fresh veggies to your sandwich.
Service Type: Quick Service, Lunch and Dinner daily

Thunder Falls Terrace

This restaurant is fun for kids because you have a great view of the splashdown of Jurassic Park ride! Not only does this place offer the best BBQ Ribs platter with mango BBQ sauce plus wraps, burgers, rotisserie chicken, and salads. Service Type: Quick Service, Lunch and Dinner daily
Price Range: From $6 to $15

Toon Lagoon Dining

Comic Strip Cafe
The walls are covered with funny comics which will distract you from the very average cafeteria-style food—Fried Chicken, Fish & Chips, Hot Dogs, Burgers, and even Asian & Italian Dishes. Tip: Skip the apple pie! There are other better desserts in the park.
Service Type: Quick Service, 11:00am to half-hour before Park Close daily

Cathy's Ice Cream

Cathy Guisewite's beloved comic character, Cathy, invites you to cool off with Sundaes, Shakes and Waffle Cones featuring Ben & Jerry's Ice Cream.

Service Type: Quick Service
Hours: 11:00am to half-hour before Park Close daily
Price Range: From $3 to $7

Blondie's: Home of the Dagwood

A gravity-defying sandwich tops the facade of this sandwich spot which offers a variety of fresh meats, cheeses, vegetables and dressings. Choose from hot dogs, made-to-order sub sandwiches and of course the famous, piled-high "Dagwood."
Service Type: Quick Service
Hours: Lunch and Dinner daily
Price Range: From $6 to $10

Marvel Super Hero Island Dining

You could literally spend hours studying the fantastic artwork of the Marvel area. Listed below are a couple of spot to satisfy a superhero's appetite. The artwork extends into the restaurants making it almost too distracting to eat!

Cafe4

The Fantastic Four's laboratory sets the scene for this dining spot offering Pizza, Spaghetti & Meatballs, Fettuccini, Meatball Subs, and Chicken Caesar Salads. You can also order whole pizzas for about $36.   This Cafe is home to the Marvel Character Dinner on select nights.
Service Type: Quick Service

Hours: 11:00 am to Park Close Daily, Character dining is Thursday-Sunday beginning at 5:00 pm.

Captain America Diner

What could be more American than Cheeseburgers? Chicken Sandwiches, Chicken Fingers, and Crispy Chicken Salads are also on the menu.
Service Type: Quick Service, 11:00 am to park closing time

6 IMPORTANT INFO TO KNOW

Before we talk about each park, lets talk about some essential elements related to visiting with kids to think about before your arrival.

My Universal Photos

Why drag a camera around with you when you can purchase a photo package to collect your memories? With "My Universal Photos," professional photographers are on hand at special photo-op locations including character zones and attractions. Photo packages can be purchased as an "Add-on" when purchasing park admissions online. Participating Locations

Universal Studios Florida™ Locations:

- On Location™ (park entrance photos)
- E.T.'s Toy Closet & Photo Spot™
- SpongeBob SquarePants Meet and Greet
- MEN IN BLACK™ Alien Attack™
- Revenge of the Mummy™
- Hollywood Rip Ride Rockit™
- Donkey Photo Op (near Shrek 4-D)
- Despicable Me Super Silly Stuff™ Store Photo Op
- Harry Potter and the Escape from Gringotts™ In-Queue Photo Op
- Meet The TRANSFORMERS Photo Op
- Roaming Universal Studios Florida™ Characters

Universal's Islands of Adventure™ Locations:

- DeFotos Expedition Photography™ (park entrance photos)
- Spider-Man™ Photo Op in Marvel® Alterniverse
- The Amazing Adventures of Spider-Man™
- The Incredible Hulk Coaster™
- Dudley Do-Right's Ripsaw Falls™
- Jurassic Park River Adventure™
- T-Rex Automated Photo Capture in Jurassic Park™
- Raptor Encounter Photo Op in Jurassic Park™
- Harry Potter and the Forbidden Journey™
- The High In The Sky Seuss Trolley Train Ride!™ In-Queue Photo Op
- The Grinch™ Seasonal Photo Op
- Roaming Islands of Adventure™ Characters (where applicable)

My Universal Photo Packages

1-Day Photo Package
Exclusively available online
Price: from $69.99 per Family

- One day of photos in the park
- Unlimited digital downloads of your theme park photos including character meet and greets and pictures at many of our most popular rides and attractions. Available at participating locations in Universal Studios Florida™, Universal's Islands of Adventure™ and Universal's Volcano Bay™
- My Universal Photos themed lanyard and card
- Discounts on My Universal Photos photo gift products both in-park and online
- View and share your photos throughout the day with the Amazing Pictures Mobile App*
- 1 4x6 and 1 5x7 photo print at time of purchase
- Exclusive pricing on park photo prints

3-Day Photo Package

Save $10 off the in-park price when you buy online and in advance.

Price: From $89.99 per family

- Up to three consecutive days of photos in the parks
- Unlimited digital downloads of your theme park photos including character meet and greets and

pictures at many of our most popular rides and attractions. Available at participating locations in Universal Studios Florida™, Universal's Islands of Adventure™ and Universal's Volcano Bay™

- My Universal Photos themed lanyard and card
- Discounts on My Universal Photos photo gift products both in-park and online
- One free 5x7 print in a folder
- One free 4x6 print valid in-park or online
- $5.00 5x7 or $10.00 8x10 prints at participating My Universal Photos locations
- $2.00 4x6 prints at participating My Universal Photos locations
- View and share your photos throughout the day with the Amazing Pictures Mobile App*View and share your photos throughout the day with the Amazing Pictures Mobile App

1 Day Photo Package at Volcano Bay

Save $10 off the in-park price when you buy online and in advance.

Price from $39.99 per family

- One day of photos in Universal's Volcano Bay™
- Unlimited digital downloads of your theme park photos from participating locations in Universal's Volcano Bay
- View and share your photos throughout the day with the Amazing Pictures Mobile App
- FYI: Shutterbuttons in Diagon Alley, Wizarding World of Harry Potter, is NOT included in My

Universal Photos packages.

What if You Have a Lost Child?

If the unthinkable happens, and your child is lost, don't panic. Team Members (employees) at Universal Orlando are trained to spot lost children. If you lose sight of your child, find the nearest Team Member. The Team Member will report the lost child and an "all points bulletin" will be issued through internal communications. The next step is to head to Guest Services which is where lost children are taken until parents arrive to claim them.

When you arrive at the parks, introduce your child to different Team Members, noting their identification. This way, your child will be less afraid and know who to talk to if they are lost. Write contact information including cell phone number and names on their arm or somewhere on the child with a Sharpie Permanent Marker. Make sure the child knows where they are marked.

Child Swap

Universal has almost perfected the procedure for parents to switch off so each can experience a ride while the other waits with their child. Child Swap is perfect for families with children who are either too small or too afraid to ride. Upon entering the ride queue, tell the Team Member that you wish to use the Child Swap option. You might even go through a shorter line! The child swap feature is a great way for adults who prefer to go through the queue with their group, but prefer not to ride. At some Child Swap locations, entertainment is provided and there is usually a changing station available.

Where to Find Shade and Solitude at the Parks

When traveling with kids and infants, finding shade and a little quiet can be very important. Since many guests do not stay onsite, getting away to the hotel for a while is not always practical. While solitude seems an unattainable experience at the parks, there are a few places to get away from the crowds.

Check your park map for the following areas.

Universal Studios Quiet Spots:

Central Park, between Hollywood and Springfield

- Animal Actors covered table seating area

- Springfield, behind Duff Brewery and Bumblebee Taco Truck

- San Francisco, table seating near the lake

- New York Library steps at the end of the lane between Jimmy Fallon and Macy's

Islands of Adventure Quiet Spots:

• Lake area Near Popeye's Bilge Rat Barges

• Port of Entry rock area at the lake

• Mythos Restaurant (in the rear near the lake)

• Seuss Landing seating area near the Green Eggs and Ham Cafe

• Marvel Super Hero Island area near the lake behind Captain America Diner

Choose a Meeting Spot

If you get separated from your party and don't have access to cell phones, arranging a meeting spot can be crucial. Here are a couple of good places for families to meet:

Universal Studios: Central Park, just outside of Hollywood and before Springfield.

Islands of Adventure: Port of Entry at the Lake near the rocks in the shadow of The Incredible Hulk Coaster.

First Aid and Facilities for Nursing Mothers

Traveling with an infant often requires special facilities. Nursing mothers need not worry. Universal has a Nursing Mothers Room at their

First Aid Stations near Guest Services at the front of each park. Each of these rooms provides a quiet, private space with a place to sit quietly. A corresponding rest room is located there with a changing station.

Family restrooms are located throughout the parks with changing stations. Most Mens and Ladies rooms also have changing tables.

Scrapes Happen

First Aid locations are located at the front of each park, near Guest Services. This is where you can get small bandage for minor scrapes, cuts or blisters.

For more serious medical matters, The Dr. P. Phillips Hospital on Turkey Lake Road will meet your medical needs and accepts insurance from out of state.

There are also clinics at chain pharmacies such as MinuteClinics at CVS Pharmacies or Walgreens Healthcare Clinics.

Walgreens Healthcare Clinics: www.walgreens.com/pharmacy/healthcare-clinic/locations.jsp

CVS MinuteClinic: www.cvs.com/minuteclinic/clinics/Florida/Orlando

Ride Evacuations

It is not unheard of for rides to stop or break down every once in a while. Most of the time, you can remain on the ride and unload in the normal fashion. However, if an evacuation of an attraction is required, guests may be required to navigate stairs, narrow walkways, or on extremely rare occasions, a ladder. In this event, staff are trained if you need assistance.

7 THE RIDES!

Insert Universal may not have an abundance of fairy princesses, but there is no lack of fun attractions for kids. What it lacks in crooning fairy princesses, it makes up for it with state-of-the-art rides, amusing shows, delightful character meet and greets and interactive play areas.

Even though every child is different, ride ratings are provided to give you an idea of how your child might respond the attractions. The following is my list of ride ratings:

G = Great for Families. Includes attractions which entertains all ages.

K = Kids Age 9 and Under. Attractions which are specifically designed for younger kids.

D = Dark. Dark rides are indoor rides with intermittent elements of darkness.

T = Best for Teens and Adults. Includes thrill rides, roller coasters, scary and dark rides.

MS = Motion Sensory. These multi-dimensional rides with filmed sequences which are not recommended for those susceptible to motion sickness or vertigo.

There are very few attractions which do not have height requirements at Universal Studios and Islands of Adventure. All attractions require an adult or taller companion if the guest is under 48" in height.

Universal Studios is segmented into these areas:

Production Central
New York
Wizarding World of Harry Potter —Diagon Alley (including London Waterfront)
World Expo (including Springfield)
Woody Woodpecker's KidZone
Hollywood

The themed lands at Islands of Adventure are a little different than those at Universal Studios. They key word at this park is adventure! The state-of-the-art rides, amusing shows and interactive play areas have won this park the title of Number One Theme Park in the World for several years! Instead of being based on solely on movies, the emphasis of this park began from legends, comics, and literature. This has been expanded to films as well. Islands of Adventure is segmented into six "islands" as follows:

Port of Entry
Marvel Super Hero Island
Toon Lagoon
Jurassic Park
The Wizarding World of Harry Potter—Hogsmeade
The Lost Continent
Seuss Landing

Tip: Wear comfortable walking shoes. This is not the time for Prada!

The Roller Coasters

Thrill seekers could find no better place than Islands of Adventure and Universal Studios with three major roller coasters and a drop ride. Note: Metal detectors have been places at these high impact rides.

FYI: You may no longer ride with a cell phone, camera or even loose change in your pockets. Wear eye glasses at your own risk of loss.

Hollywood Rip Ride Rocket

The Rockit is a thrill seekers dream attraction! This is the only roller coaster that lets you customize your ride experience. As you load into your ride vehicle, you are given the option to make a music selection for your listening pleasure while you are rocketing skyward! Your ride vehicle is also fitted with a video camera so that you may purchase a copy of your ride experience.

The Rockit is Orlando's tallest roller coaster at 17 stories high and features several exciting elements, including the world's first non-inverting loop! The ride reaches 65 mph at its top speed as it loops and curls through Production Central and even through the New York buildings!

Fun Fact: Although the Hollywood Rip Ride Rockit coaster has loops and twists, riders are never actually upside down.

Location: Universal Studios, Production Central
Rating: T
Height Requirement: 51" to 79"
Metal Detectors at this ride

Revenge of the Mummy

The Mummy, an indoor roller coaster, is my personal favorite roller coaster! It is not for the faint-hearted but it is a great coaster for anyone afraid of heights. Throughout the ride, you'll encounter a terrifying Mummy, Imhotep, forecasting your doom. You'll see a treasure room with piles of gold, swarms of scarab beetles, feel the heat of fireballs, have sudden stops and a few more surprises.

Location: Universal Studios, New York
Rating: T
Height Requirement: 48"
No bags allowed—there are temporary lockers.

The Incredible Hulk Coaster

The roar of the Hulk can be heard all over Islands of Adventure and CityWalk! The big green guy's coaster has been completely rebuilt, with new foundation supports for a smoother ride. The queue has been redesigned based on the Marvel comics character, The Incredible Hulk. Don't worry, what you love about the Hulk remains. You accelerate from zero to 40 miles per hour in two seconds and begin to experience a weightless "zero gravity" roll as you go through loops and turns.

Location: Islands Of Adventure, Marvel Super Hero Island
Height Req: 54"
Rating: T, Metal Detectors, no bags

Hagrid's Magical Creatures Motorbike Adventure

Not much is known yet about the new roller coaster at Islands of Adventure. What we do know is that it opens on June 13, 2019 on the site of the closed Dragon Challenge in Hogsmeade and that it will be a highly themed roller coaster.

Dr. Doom's Fearfall

On this drop ride, the ascend is just as dramatic and the drop! Just when you think nothing will happen, you skyrocket 185 feet into the air, then quickly drop in a series of ups and downs. A best feature of this ride is the view!
Location: Islands of Adventure, Marvel Super Hero Island
Height Requirement: 52"
Rating: T
No bags

Multi-Sensory, Multi-Dimensional Rides

Universal Studios began with the slogan, "Ride the Movies." This theme set these parks apart from other theme parks. At both of the Universal Orlando theme parks, you'll find rides with screens and filmed sequences to add to the experience.

Since some guests may be subject to motion sickness, each ride has been rated on a "Queasy Scale" of 0 to 5 (5 being the worst).

Fast & Furious: Supercharged

On this dark ride, you'll enter a bus and join Dom, Letty, Hobbs and the rest of the crew who is getting ready for a party but they need your help in apprehending a foe. You'll encounter high speed chases and see locations from the films. The attraction has a great queue with iconic vehicles to peruse.

Location: Universal Studios, San Francisco
Height Requirement: 40"
Rating: G, T, D, MS
Queasy Scale: 3

Race Through New York Starring Jimmy Fallon

This ride is a thrilling attraction which gives guests the ultimate "Tonight Show" experience. The queue has great interest for fans of The Tonight Show with exhibit cases of each host of The Tonight Show over the years. Next, you enter a "Green Room" and you are assigned a "color." Groups of guests are called by their designated color but while they wait there are tv monitors with funny clips from Jimmy Fallon's Tonight Show. There is also live entertainment by a Barber Shop quartet so the wait is not as bad as other attractions. When you color flashes, you enter the actual ride where you'll take off on a wild and action-packed race through New York City against Jimmy Fallon himself. The ride is the first attraction to feature a Virtual Line experience at Universal Studios Florida.

Location: Universal Studios, New York
Height Requirement: 40"
Rating: G, T, D, MS
Queasy Scale: 4

Despicable Me Minion Mayhem

Join Gru, Agnes, Margo and Edith for an exciting adventure as you begin your Minion training. A word of advice: Resist the banana! The attraction is fun for all ages and loads into auditorium seating which does involve movement. Stationary seating is available.

Location: Universal Studios, Production Central
Height Requirement: 40"
No Single Rider Line
Rating: G, D, T, MS
Queasy Scale: 5

Shrek 4-D

Evil Lord Farquaad has returned (in ghostly form) to kidnap Princess Fiona. Shrek and Donkey race to the rescue in this rollicking auditorium seating 4-D experience. Stationary seating is available.

Location: Universal Studios, Production Central
No Height Requirement

Rating: G, D, MS
No Single Rider Line
Queasy Scale: 3

TRANSFORMERS: The Ride-3D

At this attraction, riders get caught up in the battle between the Autobots and Decepticons. Your mission is to help Optimus Prime and Bumblebee keep the Allspark from falling into enemy hands. There are ride vehicles which seat 4 across and you will encounter film, sets, spinning, racing, and the feeling of falling.

Location: Universal Studios, Production Central
Height Requirement:
Rating: G, D, T, MS
Queasy Scale: 3

Harry Potter and the Escape from Gringotts

At this attraction, you enter the opulent lobby of Gringotts Bank on a tour, but get sidetracked by Voldemort and a dragon! The queue and lead up to the ride is great, with animatronic goblins hard at work at their desks. The queue takes you to a "lift" which takes you deep down into the cavernous underground passageways where you will encounter the good guys, bad guys and the dragon! As you climb aboard Harry Potter and the Escape from Gringotts.

Location: Universal Studios, Diagon Alley

Height Requirement: 42"
Rating: G, D, T, MS
No Universal Express Line, no bags allowed
Queasy Scale: 3

The Amazing Adventures of Spider-Man

This original park ride is a multi-sensory masterpiece and the first of its kind. The ride has won multiple awards and continues to be a favorite of all ages. The queue will keep you entertained with creative subtle comic book humor. You'll load into ride vehicles which seat 4 across. On your journey to assist Spider-Man, you will race through the streets of New York, where you encounter the diabolical villains of the Sinister Syndicate who have stolen the Statue of Liberty. Along with Spiderman, you can save the day!

Location: Islands of Adventure, Marvel Super Hero Island
Height Requirement: 40"
Rating: G, T, D, MS
Queasy Scale: 3

Skull Island—Reign of Kong

King Kong is back at Universal Orlando! The original King Kong ride, Kongfrontation, was originally at Universal Studios and closed in 2002. Skull Island is a perfect fit for the Jurassic Park area at Islands of Adventure. The queue contains witch doctors and lots of skulls to look at to keep guests entertained while waiting. This attraction is themed to the 2005 film, King Kong, starring Naomi Watts and Jack Black but is also relevant to 2017 film, Kong: Skull Island. The ride vehicles are expedition trucks using driverless technology. As you enter the structure, the action begins as our tour guides are attached by prehistoric creatures. Although the ride seems short, it's actually the longest attraction in the park.

Location: Islands of Adventure, Jurassic Park
Height Requirement: 36"
Rating: T, D, MS
Queasy Scale: 2

Tip: Look from side to side as action happens on both sides of the truck.

Harry Potter and the Forbidden Journey

As you enter Hogwarts Castle, you are experiencing two attractions in one—the Castle tour and the ride. This amazing, ground breaking attraction has won a number of awards and is a favorite ride whether a Potter fan or not! First, as you go through the queue, you are touring Hogwarts Castle; the dungeons, the dark arts classroom, portrait gallery and the Gryffindor common room. As you board the "enchanted bench" Hermione sends you through the Floo Network. On your way to the Quidditch Pitch, you encounter a dragon, dementors, giant spiders and more.

Location: Islands of Adventure, Hogsmeade
Height Requirement: 48"
Rating: T, D, MS
No bags allowed
Queasy Scale: 5+

Warning: This attraction severely affects anyone prone to Vertigo or motion sickness. It is off the queasy scale!

The Simpsons Ride™

Everything goes haywire when the Simpsons board a new ride, but little do they know that it's been sabotaged by Sideshow Bob! The queue on this ride is fantastic for fans of the show, The Simpsons. Motion sickness is possible on this ride.
Location: Universal Studios, Springfield
Height Requirement: 40"
Rating: G, D, MS
Queasy Scale: 5

Getting Wet: The Water Rides

In Florida, the tropical climate means heat and humidity. Having a few water rides adds a fun element and guests get a chance to cool off.

Best times to ride water rides:

First thing in the morning so you have a chance to dry off

Right before lunch, so you can head back to the hotel to change

At the end of the day so that you're not walking around in wet clothes all day.

Tip: Pack a pair of flip flops and change of clothes in a backpack to change into for the wet rides to keep athletic shoes dry. Once your socks get wet, they won't dry and there are surprisingly few socks for sale in gift shops.

Dudley Do-Right's Ripsaw Falls®

Join our Canadian hero on his quest to rescue Nell from Snidely Whiplash on this fun flume ride with a steep drop at the end. Make no mistake, and I am not exaggerating, you will get wet!

Location: Islands of Adventure, Toon Lagoon
Height Requirement: 44"
Rating: G

Popeye & Bluto's Bilge-Rat Barges®

Dastardly Bluto is at it again and Popeye is here to save the day. This exceptional white-water rafting ride may be the best ride of its kind in the world! There are multiple ways to get wet, from an 18-foot waterfall, water cannons and splash downs. On this ride, you will get wet!

Location: Islands of Adventure, Toon Lagoon

Height Requirement: 42"
Rating: G

Jurassic Park River Adventure

Whether or not you remember the original Jurassic Park film, you'll enjoy this thrilling river raft adventure. It begins with a leisurely ride through the jungles of Jurassic Park, seeing plant eating dinosaurs in their natural habitats. Then something goes wrong and you're taken off course and into the restricted Raptor Containment Area and the only escape from the T-Rex is an 85-foot plunge. There is a very good chance of getting wet on this ride.
Location: Islands of Adventure, Jurassic Park
Height Requirement: 42"
Rating: G

Fun for Kids and Adults

Throughout the two parks, there are many rides that provide entertainment for the whole family!

The Hogwarts Express—King's Cross Station

The magic began for Harry and for you too when you board the Hogwarts Express at King's Cross Station where after walking through a brick wall onto Platform 9 ¾, you begin your journey to

Hogwarts Castle. Along the way, you'll encounter Harry, Hermione, Ron and a couple of dementors! This train ride takes you to Hogsmeade in Islands of Adventure.

Location: Universal Studios, London Waterfront
No Height Requirement
Rating: G
No Universal Express Line

You must have Park-to-Park access in order to ride.

MEN IN BLACK™ Alien Attack™

Begin your MIB training on this ride where you blast aliens and save the planet! You'll take aim, shoot and even spin and compete for the high score! The setting is the 1964 World's Fair exhibit "The Universe and You."

Location: Universal Studios, World Expo
Height Requirement: 42"
Rating: G, T
No Bags Allowed

Kang & Kodos' Twirl 'n' Hurl

You might not want to fuel up at Fast Food Boulevard before riding this gently "twirling" ride. Set in the land of the Simpsons, this Alien ride's theme will add a giggle to your day.

Location: Universal Studios, Springfield
No Height Requirement
Rating: K, G

Woody Woodpecker's Nuthouse Coaster®

This is the most gentle coaster ride you will find!
It is perfect coaster for small kids.
Location: Universal Studios, Woody Woodpeckers
KidZone
Height Requirement: 36"
Rating: K, G

E.T. Adventure®

A flying bicycle is your ride vehicle on this
original park ride (the only one left). You escape
with E. T. and join him in a celebration on his home
planet. Tip: Watch the movie with your kids before
you come!

Location: Universal Studios, Woody Woodpecker's
KidZone
Height Requirement: 34"
Rating: K, G

Pteranodon Flyers

This two seat ride is a gentle hang gliding
experience with incredible views. This attraction is
designed for children 36" to 56" in height. Guests
over 56" in height must be accompanied by a child

meeting the 36" to 56" height requirement. Children between 36"-56" must be accompanied by a Supervising Companion.

Location: Islands of Adventure, Jurassic Park
Height Requirement: 36"-56" (over 56" must accompany a child)
Rated: K

Storm Force Accelatron

Despite it's menacing appearance, this Marvel themed ride based on X-Men's Storm is a purple and gold vehicle attraction which can be compared to a "tea cup ride." You'll giggle and smile and twirl and twirl.

Location: Islands of Adventure, Marvel Super Hero Island
No Height Requirement
Rating: K, G

Flight of the Hippogriff

This Harry Potter themed ride is a fun small roller coaster with an amazing queue with the only view of Hagrid's Cabin and Buckbeak.

Location: Islands of Adventure, Hogsmeade
Height Requirement: 36"
Rating: K, G

The Cat in the Hat

This ride, based on the famous book about the intrusive cat and his mischievous cohorts, will delight as it swings and turns through the pages of the book of the same name.

Location: Islands of Adventure, Seuss Landing
Height Requirement: 36"
Rating: K, G

One Fish, Two Fish, Red Fish, Blue Fish

Yet another ride based on the whimsical musings of the Dr. Seuss book of the same name, this is a colorful "Dumbo" style ride with a small chance getting wet!

Location: Islands of Adventure, Seuss Landing
No Height Requirement
Rating: K

Car-o-Seuss-el

Much more than your average carousel, this circling collection of creative creatures will delight even the grumpiest of guests!

Location: Islands of Adventure, Seuss Landing
No Height Requirement
Rating: K, G

The High in the Sky Seuss Trolley Train Ride!

Take a break from the regular park rides, with a delightful high in the sky train ride. The two separate tracks have a small differences and one track goes through Circus McGurkus Cafe Stoo-pendous™ letting you wave at the guests dining below. The ride gives excellent views of the park.

Location: Islands of Adventure, Seuss Landing
Height Requirement: 40"
Rating: K, G

8 SHOWS AND CHARACTERS

Universal Orlando is one of the best places to be met and greeted by characters! The characters are easily accessible without the tremendous lines which are found at Disney. Some popular characters are Sponge Bob, Marvel Super Heroes, Dr. Seuss characters, the Minions, the Simpsons, Scooby and Shaggy, Marilyn Monroe, Betty Boop and more!

Where to Meet Characters

Most people traveling with kids are looking for characters. The good new is that characters are not only found at designated character zones, but also at shows, parades and at some attractions.

Attractions with Characters

Despicable Me Minion Mayhem: Minions occasionally greet exiting guests.

Race Through New York Starring Jimmy Fallon: #Panda occasionally meets guests

Revenge of the Mummy: Stilt walking Pharoah's occasionally greet guests

Shows and Parades with Character Greetings
Consult park maps and signage for show times

At Universal Studios:

The Blues Brothers Show: New York

The Tales of Beedle the Bard: Diagon Alley

Celestina Warbeck and the Banshees: Diagon Alley Animal Actors on Location! Woody Woodpecker's KidZone—Animal occasionally greet guests

A Day in the Park with Barney: Woody Woodpecker's KidZone—Barney & B. J. greet guests after the show.

Universal's Superstar Parade: The parade begins and ends in Hollywood. Lots of Character greetings including the Minions, SpongeBob and Dora the Explorer at the end of the parade.

At Islands of Adventure:

Frog Choir: Hogsmeade

Triwizard Spirit Rally: Hogsmeade

Oh! The Stories You'll Hear!: Seuss Landing. Meet the Cat in the Hat, Thing 1 & 2, Sam I am, the Grinch and the Lorax

Universal Studios Character Encounters

Meet the Transformers: Production Central. Meet Optimus Prime, Megatron and Bumblebee

Hello Kitty: Production Central. Kitty White occasionally greets guests.

The Simpsons Character Zone: Meet Bart, Lisa, Homer, Marge and Sideshow Bob

Meet SpongeBob Square Pants: Woody Woodpecker's Kidzone. Patrick and Bob greet guests at the Sponge Bob store.

Meet Shrek and Donkey: Production Central.

Hollywood Character Zone: Hollywood. Meet Lucille Ball, Marilyn Monroe, Shaggy and Scooby, Betty Boop, Curious George, Woody Woodpecker,

Doc Brown, Beetlejuice and more.

Islands of Adventure Character Encounters

Raptor Encounter: Jurassic Park. Meet the newest raptor, Blue. This is my favorite character encounter but may be a little to loud and scary for the very young.

Spider-Man Appearing at the Alterniverse Store: Marvel Super Hero Island.

Meet Marvel Super Heroes: Marvel Super Hero Island. If you listen, you'll hear S.H.I.E.L.D. calling for agents to combat villains in the area. Occasionally, the heroes ride in on 4-wheel vehicles. Meet Classic Comic Book Characters: Toon Lagoon. Popeye, Olive, Betty Boop and Beetle Baily greet guests throughout the day.

CityWalk Character Encounters

There are a few unexpected establishments at CityWalk which feature character encounters.

Blue Man Group—The Blue Men greet guests for photos after each performance.

Bubba Gump Shrimp Co. Restaurant—the Shrimp Mascot greets restaurant guests.

Toothsome Chocolate Emporium and Savory Feast Kitchen—As if the milkshakes weren't a giant draw, guests can also meet Dr. Penelope and her robot companion, Jacques.

9 PLAY AREAS IN THE PARKS

Insert Parents often feel that their kids should ride every ride in the park. Sometimes, kids need a little time to unwind and let loose after all that time waiting in lines. Universal Orlando has some great interactive play areas that let kids do just that!

Play Areas at Universal Studios

Barney's Backyard

Barney's Backyard is a woodsy indoor space which is perfect place for little ones to play. What's great about this playground is that it is out of the sun! There are hands-on experiences, BJ's Express train and step-on stones and giant wind chimes. There's a treehouse, slides , splash and sand area.
Location: Universal Studios, Woody Woodpeckers KidZone

Curious George Goes to Town

If you want a variety of activities, this is the place. The colorful Animal Show tent has plenty of play activities for toddlers. The "town" has cartoon buildings to explore. There are lots of water fountains and water play at this location to cool off. One of the best parts of this area is Man in the Big Yellow Hat's Ball Factory where soft balls can be launched, thrown or blasted at family and friends. Click here for a Ball Factory Youtube video.
Location: Universal Studios, Woody Woodpeckers KidZone

Fievel's Playland

Universal has its own big eared mouse and his name is Fievel Mousekewitz! Kids can run around, climb and jump through this outdoor playground with oversized props from the films An American Tail and Fievel Goes West. Kids can also cool off on a little know attraction—a 200-foot long water slide.
Location: Universal Studios, Woody Woodpeckers KidZone
Play Areas at Islands of Adventure

If I Ran the Zoo

Toddlers will be delighted with this interactive multi-level playground, complete with a tube slide. Kids can turn a crank, spin a wheel, and step on pedals to make creatures pop out and play peek and boo!

Location: Islands of Adventure, Seuss Landing

Me Ship, The Olive

Popeye is only too happy to offer his ship as a three-story play area for kids. On its decks are great views, passageways and slides. On the second deck, there are water cannons to squirt passengers riding Popeye & Bluto's Bilge-Rat Barges.
Location: Islands of Adventure, Toon Lagoon

Jurassic Park Discovery Center

This is one of the best and most overlooked attractions at Islands of Adventure. At the Jurassic Park Discovery Center, you are entering a science and education center with informative exhibits and displays geared to children and adults. The two story building features a massive T-rex and other dinosaur skeletons and displays.

Among the interactive activities offered, you can test your DNA to see what kind of dinosaur you would be, pet a baby dinosaur and you might even get to see baby raptors hatch and name them!
Location: Islands of Adventure, Jurassic Park

Camp Jurassic

In this prehistoric playground, kids can explore secret caves and wander through a mysterious amber mine. Adventurous guests can climb up and down dinosaur capture nets, play on a variety of themed slides, and negotiate suspension bridges.

Take a walk down Thunder Lizard Trail and make the ground rumble with the roar of dinosaurs. Adults and kids can join in water cannon fights in the containment paddock.
Location: Islands of Adventure, Jurassic Park

Play Areas at Volcano Bay Water Park

Note: Parental supervision is required in all areas of Volcano Bay Water Park.

Tot Tiki Reef

Tot Tiki Reef is the best spot for toddlers at Volcano Bay. There are tot sized slides, a mini volcano, and lots of spraying fountains and spraying whales that will keep little ones entertained for hours.

Runnamukka Reef

This whimsical play structure has bubbling geysers, water guns, slides and dump cups. There are bamboo sea creatures providing much needed shade. This is also a great place to spend time while waiting on Tapu Tapu.

The Reef

The Reef is a great area for relaxing in between rides or while waiting for your turn on one of the water slides.   The is a great place to watch guests take the Ko'okiri Body Plunge™ from the comfort of this peaceful leisure pool. A clear plexi tube shoots straight through the 5.5-foot deep shallows, which feature a waterfall. The Reef is set beside Waterfall Cove. It's a nice place for some leisurely swimming for bigger kids.

10 YOUR IMAGINATION RUNS LOOSE IN THE LAND OF DR. SEUSS

At perhaps the most whimsical of all theme park lands in Florida, who better to entertain kids than Dr. Seuss! In this enchanted land you'll find amusing creatures, lighthearted designs, delicious delectables, and the mirthful musings of Dr. Seuss around every turn.

This land is made up of rides, playgrounds, shops, fanciful eateries and it's topped off with the show, Oh! The Stories You'll Hear! and the holiday celebration, Grinchmas!

Seuss Landing Attractions

The Cat in the Hat

The star of the show is a very tall cat
He abides in the structure under the hat
With Thing One and Thing Two
Who Knows what they'll do

This dark ride swings you this way and that
So you'll surely love The Cat in the Hat!

One Fish, Two Fish, Red Fish, Blue Fish

Based on a favorite story of Dr. Seuss
About fish, one red and two blueish
It spins around and smiles about
And when you see water—duck!
Or you'll be out of luck!
Fish fountains squirt here and there
And if you want to stay dry—beware!

Caro-Seuss-el

Around and around, with whimsical sounds;
Creative creatures you'll ride, with friends and
family at your side.
Under Horton, we ride, and mop tops aside;
You're in for a treat, 'cause this ride is really neat!
Pull back on the reigns and give the ears a wiggle;
A ride on Car-o-Seuss-el will give you a giggle!

The High in the Sky Seuss Trolley Train Ride!

A train of two tracks, of which whimsy smacks!
The colorful musings of Dr. Seuss set your
inhibitions aside .
Inside and above Circus McGurkus Cafe Stoo-
pendous™ you'll ride;
To wave at diners whose smiles are wide!
You'll learn the tale of Sneetches,
Until the brake screeches!

Oh the Stories You'll Hear!

Hear the tales of strange creatures;
Which this Dr. Seuss show features.
The stories unfold by a teller of rhymes
About characters of which you've heard many times.
The Lorax and friends
Always bring smiles in the end.

Seuss Shopping

Cats, Hats & Things

Themed toys and gifts,
And T-shirts galore,
Thing One and Thing Two
Merchandise and More!

All the Books You Can Read

The gift of reading
With Dr. Seuss' collection
DVD's, toys and clothes
Are here for the taking.

Mulberry Street Store

Hat's and wigs, toys and glasses
From the Grinch to the Cat
Buy your stuff here
And you'll never look back!

Dr. Seuss Eateries

Snookers and Snookers Sweet Candy Cookers

Adults and Kids cannot resist
The sugary confections which within exist
From fudge, candy and snacks
Too tempting to walk past!

Circus McGurkus Cafe Stoo-pendous™

Fried Chicken, Pizza, and Spaghetti
Everything is on the menu
When your hunger is ready!

Green Eggs and Ham™ Cafe

The most famous dish
Among others on the menu is stacked
With toothsome delights, but it's only open
When the park is packed.

Hop On Pop™ Ice Cream Shop

Ice Cream flavors pop
And frozen concoctions abound
In this delectable ice cream shop!

Moose Juice, Goose Juice

Both refreshing and cooling,
Whether frozen or not
Both are healthy and healing!

Tip: See Chapter 4 for more information on Seuss Landing Dining establishments.

Tip: A popular part of Universal's Christmas celebration, Grinchmas, takes place in Seuss Landing in December.

11 THE WIZARDING WORLD OF HARRY POTTER

There cannot be a book about Universal Orlando that doesn't single out the single most creative example of literature and films, the works of J. K. Rowling!   This enchanted land of witches and wizards has been entertaining kids of all ages since it opened in 2010.   Diagon Alley and Hogsmeade, linked by the Hogwarts Express create the most immersive and imaginative land of any theme park!

Hogsmeade is located in Islands of Adventure
Diagon Alley is located in Universal Studios

Note: you must purchase Park to Park tickets to ride the Hogwarts Express to travel between parks.

The Wizarding World of Harry Potter—Hogsmeade

As you approach Hogsmeade at Islands of Adventure, the towering facade of Hogwarts looms ahead. This has become the iconic centerpiece of Universal Orlando. The castle is the home for basically two attractions. The first one is the castle tour. The second is an award winning, groundbreaking, state of the art multi-sensory, multi-dimensional ride.

The Castle Tour

For young guests or those susceptible to motion sickness, opting for the castle tour is your best bet. Tell the attraction attendant that you're interested in the tour. If it's not too busy, you may have a guided tour by a "Hogwarts student." If it is a busy time, you can walk through the queue at your own pace. The Castle Tour is basically just taking your time to walk through the queue and notice all of the fantastic details.

You enter through the dungeons, and pass several statues and the Potions class room until you come upon the Gryphon which was stationed outside Dumbledore's office in the films. Dumbledore is in but has a warning for visitors of the castle. Next, explore the dark arts classroom and the Gryffindor common room. Be sure to keep your eyes open for the portrait gallery as the founders of Hogwarts have a heated discussion, the Fat Lady who cheers for Gryffindor, and the Sorting Hat.

Harry Potter and the Forbidden Journey

As you enter the castle, you'll see all of the sights described above. At the end of the queue you'll reach the "Room of Requirement" where you'll board "enchanted benches." Hermione sends you off through the Floo Network and then you are off on a flying adventure through the grounds of Hogwarts where you'll be chased by a dragon, haunted by Dementors and join Harry and Ron on the Quidditch Pitch! The ride vehicles are powered into motion by use of Kuka-Arm technology. This ground breaking ride uses a combination of 3D film screens and actual sets.

Hagrid's Magical Creatures Motorbike Adventure

A new roller coaster opens on June 13, 2019. The theme is based on the lovable Hagrid combined with a little bit of the Fantastic Beasts and Where to Find them films. Expect the longest lines in the parks.

Flight of the Hippogriff

Step into Hagrid's territory as you enter the queue for this "kiddie" roller coaster. It may be a kids' ride, but you'll probably find more adult Harry Potter fans in line. In the queue you get a great view of Hagrid's cabin and on the ride, you'll come face to face with Buckbeak, the hippogriff as you ascend on the tracks. It's a fun and fast ride which gives you a spectacular view of the castle and the rest of the park. Be sure to bow to Buckbeak!

The Wizarding World of Harry Potter— Diagon Alley

Harry Potter and the Escape from Gringotts

This attraction combines a fantastic queue experience, motion simulation technology, film and roller coaster tracks to create an innovative and immersive experience. You enter through Gringotts, the goblin bank, and pass the many goblin clerks who aren't necessarily happy to have Muggle visitors. As you progress, notice the goblin names on office doors and newspaper headlines. Then you'll enter the lift which "descends" into the depths as you go on search through the vaults. On the ride you'll meet Bill Weasley, Voldemort, Bellatrix LeStrange, Harry, Ron, Hermione and of course, the dragon!

Hogwarts Express—Hogsmeade Station and King's Cross

Whether you are in Hogsmeade or the London

Waterfront, you will be thrilled to run into Harry, Ron and Hermione on this authentic train ride that takes you from Platform 9 3/4 to Hogsmeade and back again. Park-to-park admission is required to ride and it's a different experience each way.

The Shows

Ollivanders—In Diagon Alley and Hogsmeade

An attraction which kids simply can't miss is "The Wand Chooses the Wizard Ceremony" at Ollivanders. A group of no more than 25 people are shown into a Wand Showroom. The attending wizard chooses a prospective "wizard" from the group at random. The wizard is then asked to perform several spells until the perfect wand is found. Harry Potter and the Sorcerer's Stone fans shouldn't miss this show. Tip: Diagon Alley is a better location to see this show because there is no shade to wait in Hogsmeade. If you want to attend the Hogsmeade location, go first thing in the morning. Children age 10-13 are often chosen for the ceremony.
Location: Hogsmeade and Diagon Alley

Tales of Beedle the Bard

Wonderfully elaborate puppet shows are performed daily in the Carkitt Market section of Diagon Alley. The shows usually alternates between two stories from the storybook of the same name. These tales were made famous by the book and film,

Harry Potter and the Deathly Hallows. One puppet show often performed is titled, The Fountain of Fair Fortune. Another is titled, The Tale of the Three Brothers.
Location: Carkitt Market Stage

Celestina Warbeck and the Banshees

Molly Weasley's favorite wizarding songstress, Celestina Warbeck entertains daily on the Carkitt Market stage with alternating musical selections with special songs during the holidays. She and her dancing warblers, The Banshees, often pull an unsuspecting guest up from the crowd to the stage to be serenaded.
Location: Carkitt Market Stage

The Frog Choir
Hogwarts students are on hand to give a vocal performance featuring their musically croaking toads. The students represent each house of Hogwarts—Gryffindor, Slytherin, Hufflepuff and Ravenclaw. The students are available for photos with guests after the performances.
Location: Hogsmeade Stage

TriWizard Spirit Rally

This is a Hogwarts style pep rally, to cheer on the visiting students vying for the TriWizard Cup. The Durmstrang gentlemen perform an acrobatic show which precedes the ballet moves of the enchanting ladies of Beauxbatons Academy as they

lead the excitement for the Triwizard Tournament. The students are available for photos with guests after the performance.
Location: Hogsmeade Stage

Tastes of the Wizarding World

When you are ready for a snack or a meal, Diagon Alley and Hogsmeade are great places to be. These parts of the wizarding world are free of American soft drinks and commercial endorsements. The only ads you will see are from the wizarding world. Don't expect to purchase a Coke or Sprite here.

If there was one thing to taste which represents the wizarding world, it is Butterbeer. In Hogsmeade, it's available from one of the two big red kegs or at The Hogs Head Pub. In Diagon Alley, it is available at The Leaky Cauldron, The Hopping Pot, and The Fountain of Fair Fortune. Other beverages to enjoy are Otter's Fizzy Orange Juice, Fishy Green Ale (a version of bubble tea), Peachtree Fizzing Tea, Tongue Tying Lemon Squash and Pumpkin Juice.

At Eternelle's Elixers of Life, you can purchase Gilly Water (which is just bottled water) and choose from four additional elixirs to add:

Fire Protection Potion
Babbling Beverage
Draught of Peace

Elixir to Induce Euphoria
Location: Diagon Alley
Florean Fortescue's Ice Cream Parlour

As the Florida heat intensifies, a stop in at Harry's favorite ice cream parlour is exactly what the wizard doctor ordered. Florean's offers a deliciously unique array of flavors in soft serve and hard packed ice creams. The showpiece flavor is Butterbeer Ice Cream. Ice cream is served here in cups, waffle cones, and plastic souvenir sundae glasses. The soft serve has a magical element which creates a striped effect for extra flavour. A single order can contain two different flavors, and you can add unusual toppings like shortbread crumbles and meringue pieces. There are also specialty sundaes served in a souvenir glass. Try Harry's favorite flavour, Strawberry Peanut Butter. It is better than it sounds!

Soft serve flavors:

Banana
Chocolate
Granny Smith
Mint
Pistachio
Vanilla
Orange Marmalade
Toffee
Toffee Apple
Strawberries & Cream

Hard pack flavors:

Chocolate Chili
Apple Crumble
Vanilla
Salted Caramel Blondie
Chocolate
Clotted Cream
Earl Grey & Lavender
Sticky Toffee Pudding
Raspberry & Chocolate
Strawberry Peanut Butter
Location: Diagon Alley

The Leaky Cauldron

This restaurant is based on Harry's first entrance through the brick wall into the wizarding world. It is a quick service restaurant but with its own special menu of British fare. Breakfast, lunch and dinner are served here. Kids meals are available and there are a variety of desserts available including Butterbeer Potted Cream. There are a few American choices, but if you'd like to try British fare, there is Cottage Pie, Bangers and Mash or Toad in a Hole, and more.
Location: Diagon Alley

The Three Broomsticks

This original wizarding world restaurant was first seen in the film, Harry Potter and the Prisoner of Azkaban and it is where Harry tried Butterbeer

for the first time. The restaurant features a menu with a mix of British fare and American favorites. You can get anything from Shepherd's Pie to Barbecued Ribs. The Great Feast has smoked chicken, ribs, salad, fresh vegetables, roasted potatoes and corn on the cob. It can feed a large family. Tip: From time to time, shadows of house elves can be seen in the rafters shuffling their brooms. The restaurant is adjacent to the Hogs Head Pub.
Location: Diagon Alley

Wizard Sweets

Honeydukes is the original sweets shop in Hogsmeade. This is the place to purchase chocolate frogs, Bertie Botts Every Flavored Beans, sugar quills, chocolate wands and peppermint toads. Sweets are also available in Weasley's Wizard Wheezes and at Sugarplums in the Carkitt Market area of Diagon Alley.

Tip: Butterbeer flavour can be enjoyed in 5 different ways: Original, frozen, hot Butterbeer (seasonal), Butterbeer fudge, and Butterbeer potted cream

Shopping for Wizarding Supplies

Diagon Alley and Hogsmeade are a Potter fan's souvenir paradise. You can buy items such as school robes, quidditch jerseys, broomsticks, quills, and last but never least, interactive wands. If you plan to take part is casting spells, an interactive wand should be your first purchase.

Wands can be purchased at either location of Ollivanders, on street carts, or at Gregorovitch Wands in Diagon Alley. Character wand may be purchased which are replicas from characters in the books and films. Each wand comes with a map showing all of the spell locations.

In Hogsmeade, wizarding supplies can be purchased at Owl Post, Dervish and Bangs, and Filch's Emporium of Confiscated Goods.

In Diagon Alley, souvenirs are available at Quality Quidditch Supplies, Madam Malkin's Robes for all Occasions, Globus Mundi, Gringotts Money Exchange, Wiseacre's Wizarding Equipment, Scribulus and Magical Menagerie.

Knockturn Alley

Just past the Leaky Cauldron is a dark and cold alleyway called Knockturn Alley, which is a haven for dark wizards. There are several creative spell casting spots in Knockturn Alley as well as Borgin and Burkes, a shop with such items as crystal skulls, dark wizard wear and death eater masks.
Location: Diagon Alley

Casting Spells

The most unique experience of any theme park in the world is to be had at Diagon Alley and Hogsmeade. With the interactive wands available for purchase, guests can cast spells at designated spell locations. Included with your wand is a map outlining the spell locations and directions for spell casting. If you have trouble achieving the magic, there is usually a Team Member dressed in wizard attire, ready to help. Tip: Don't miss the Knockturn Alley spells because they are some of the best! But hold on to your wand. A wizard never gives away his wand!

Characters Greetings

J. K. Rowling, who has creative control at the wizarding world, and because of this, we will never see a Harry Potter, Hermione or Dumbledore character meet and greet. There are a few places to meet some wizard characters.

Gringott's Money Exchange

Around the corner from Gringott's iconic bank building, Gringott's Money Exchange is the place where Muggles can trade their Muggle currency for Wizard Cash. An interactive Goblin clerk will answer questions, although sometimes rather impatiently. You can also buy chocolate gold galleons.
Location: Diagon Alley

Tip: Ask the goblin clerk if he is a house elf! You'll get a surprising answer.

The Knight Bus

Stan Shunpike is your Knight Bus conductor and his interactive companion, Dreg Head will have an interactive conversation with you and he might even let you take a look inside the bus.
Location: London Waterfront

Exploring London

The London Waterfront is a facade which hides Diagon Alley from unsuspecting Muggles. The above mentioned night bus is the centerpiece of the area, but there are a few things to point out.

No. 12 Grimmauld Place

This is the ancestral home of the dark wizarding family, Black and home to Sirius Black, Harry Potter's Godfather and his grumpy house elf, Kreacher. Tip: Look up at the second floor window to see Kreacher look out every few minutes.

The Red Phone Booth

The iconic red phone booth of London has a magical purpose. Tip: Dial the word MAGIC and listen. You might get a magical message.

The Leaky Cauldron Sign

"The sign was so faded that Muggles tended not to notice it." This is the Leaky Cauldron's first mention in the book, Harry Potter and the Sorcerer's Stone. The same is true at the London Waterfront. Most guests walk right past and do not notice it. It's right across from the red phone booth.

London Taxi Stands

There are two green Cab shelters in London. One sells British merchandise. The other sells sodas, crisps, and amazing jacket potatoes (loaded baked potatoes).

For the most detailed and up to date information about The Wizarding World of Harry Potter at Universal Orlando, get my Amazon book, *Geek's Guide to the Wizarding World of Harry Potter at Universal Orlando.*

12 CITYWALK ATTRACTIONS AND ENTERTAINMENT

Hollywood Drive-in Golf

Test your putting skills with CityWalk own mini golf course. Choose between 18 or 36 holes. The south side is Invaders from Planet Putt. The course is complete with cows, bugs and little green aliens. The north side is The Haunting of Ghostly Greens and is great fun at night with neon lighting.

Hollywood Drive-in Golf is open seven days a week from 9am to 2am.

Rates:

18 Holes
Adult - $13.62
Child - $11.92

36 Holes
Adult - $25.92
Child - $22.32

FYI: Parking is free after 6pm except during certain annual events.

Blue Man Group

One of the most highly regarded shows in Orlando is Blue Man Group. It's a multi-sensory experience featuring music, dance, special effects and comedy. It is well worth a night out to experience the outrageous and entertaining shenanigans of the Blue Men.

Be a Blue Man VIP!

The Blue Man Group offers an exclusive experience for about $200 per adult and $150 per child (ages 3-9).

Here's what's included in the VIP Experience Ticket:

One hour before the show, you'll get an exclusive behind-the-scenes tour of the theater and have the chance to play a Blue Man Group instrument. Plus, you'll get the best seats in the house, souvenir popcorn and soda, a private meet-and-greet with a Blue Man and more.

FYI: Blue Man Group discounted tickets are available for annual passholders and onsite guests.

Universal Cinemark Theaters

What do you do if it's raining? Take your pick of one of the latest movies at at the newly rebranded Universal Cinemark, formerly AMC Universal Cineplex 20. This is not your average movie theater. Relax in comfort in the all-stadium seating with high backed rocking chairs. The concession stands serve hot foods like pizza and fries, plus a full liquor bar featuring beer and wine.

13 ANNUAL EVENTS

Throughout the year, scheduled annual events draw locals and guests from abroad. Some of these events require a separate ticket which not included in regular park passes. Not all of these events are appropriate for children, but most of them are. Even the onsite hotels host adult themed annual events such as Velvet Sessions at the Hard Rock and Harbour Nights at the Portofino.

Rock the Universe

Rock the Universe is an annual event occurs on February 1 and 2, 2019. This event is Florida's biggest Christian music festival. It's an entire weekend of great music, faith, and fist-pumping Christian rock music. This event requires separate admission fees. Universal Studios closes early on days when this event is scheduled.

Mardi Gras Celebrations

Mardi Gras is an annual event which is wonderful for kids. It occurs in late winter and early spring from February 9 through April 4, 2019 at Universal Studios Florida. The celebration's theme is based on the famous New Orleans Mardi Gras celebration. The celebrations include parades with extravagantly lit floats with riders tossing beads to the crowds. Annual passholders have a special viewing area for the parades. The viewing area is available one hour prior to parade start.

French Quarter style food is sold at special pavilions in the New York section as well as special cocktails. Street performers add the fun experience. These characters include court jesters and stilt walkers which greet and entertain guests.
A concert series with headlining artists perform on select nights. Admission is included with Universal Studios park admission. Seasonal annual passholders are blocked out for this event.

Summer Concert Series

On select Saturday nights in June and July, Universal Studios offers some of the leading music stars perform live in the Summer Concert Series. The best part is that these concerts are included in the price of admission. Past artists include headliners like Kelly Clarkson, One Direction, Trace Atkins, Heart and the B-52's. Sign up for emails on the Universal Orlando site to receive updates. Seasonal passholders are blocked out for this event.

Fall Concert Series

The Fall Concert Series happens on weekend nights in November. Headlining artists in the past included Jason Derulo, Colbie Caillat, and Carly Rae Jepsen. Admission is included with park admission to Universal Studios. Seasonal Annual Passholders are blocked out for this event.

Halloween Horror Nights

The most popular of these annual events by far is Halloween Horror Nights. Although there are no age restrictions, this event gets a Rating of T for Terror! During Halloween Horror Nights, Universal Studios becomes transformed to the scariest place on Earth! In 2019, the event will be held on select nights from September 6 through November 2. This event requires a separate admission ticket. The event is held on several nights, usually Thursday through Sunday nights, from mid September to the beginning of November.

There are scare zones which have large props, stages and wandering creepy characters. "Haunted" houses are based on popular horror movies and television shows. Universal Studios closes at 5:00pm on days when this event is scheduled. This event may sell out so get your tickets early if you are sure you are going to attend and arrive early.

For smaller crowds, visit near the beginning of the season and avoid weekends. Arrive at the event as soon as the gates open to beat the crowds who want to go after dark. The daylight only affects the scariness of scare zones. Thursdays are the least crowded days.

Tip: Halloween Horror Nights closes at 2:00 a.m., this is a great time to stay onsite at an onsite resort.

This event is not recommended for children under the age of 13, but teens will love it. The scare actors assume if you are there, you want to be scared so small children are not spared. If you plan to attend, purchasing Universal Express is recommended because the wait times for the different scare houses can reach more than two hours. This event is extremely popular with locals and Florida residents so be prepared for crowds.

Holidays Celebrations at Universal Orlando

Grinchmas

The Grinchmas holiday celebration is a fantastic time to take kids to Universal's Islands of Adventure. A highlight of the annual event is the Grinchmas character breakfast held at Seuss Landing's restaurant, Circus McGurkus Cafe Stoopendous. A stage show live version of "How The

Grinch Stole Christmas" is shown each day and there are multiple opportunities for character meet and greets throughout Seuss Landing.

Macy's Holiday Parade

The Macy's annual holiday parade is a favorite annual event at Universal Studios. It features character floats, marching bands, and street performers. The Despicable Me Minions are the star of this parade as well as many other Universal characters and the parade also features exclusive Macy's balloons. Annual passholders have an opportunity to take part in the parades by being balloon handlers. Seasonal annual passholders are blocked out for this event.

Christmas in the Wizarding World of Harry Potter

Christmas in The Wizarding World of Harry Potter™ debuted in 2017 in both Hogsmeade and Diagon Alley. To the delight of Harry Potter fans, the annual celebration features holiday decorations, special holiday sweet treats and drinks, a holiday menu at The Three Broomsticks and Christmas themed shows performed by the Frog Choir at Hogsmeade and Celestina Warbeck in Diagon Alley.

A great favorite of this event is the nightly lights show which is projected onto Hogwarts Castle. The show features musically themed lights, projected images and fireworks.

Tip: Get everyone a Hot Butterbeer to sip while enjoying the light show!

Eve—A New Year's Eve Celebration

Eve is a holiday celebration which takes place on New Year's Eve at CityWalk. There is a charge for admission which includes some food and beverages. Kids are welcome at most of the event with the exception of a few of the bars which ask that 21 and older only guests after 11pm. The event includes dance parties, fireworks and more. This is an event enjoyed less by young kids but okay for teens.

14 TOURING PLANS

ThrWhether you are visiting Universal Orlando for one day or five, having a plan will save you time and frustration caused by long lines and tired kids. There are plenty of touring guides out there and they basically say the same thing:

- Arrive early to beat the crowds.
- Head straight to the newest and most popular rides first.
- Take a rest at mid-day and return to the hotel.
- Ride the popular rides again in the evening when the crowds are lighter.

If you learn one thing from this book, it should be—arrive early! This is the best way to beat the crowds and see as much as you can. This strategy works at any theme park you may visit. My touring plans are very specific. Here are some touring plans and tips to help plan a great strategy for maximizing fun and minimizing frustration.

Tip: Download the ebook version of this book to your Amazon Kindle app on your smart phone so you can have this information at your fingertips! Also download the Universal Orlando App.   It has current park hours, show times and wait times.

The VIP Experience

You don't have to be a VIP to tour like one. The VIP Experience includes a guided tour with your own personal tour guide for five or seven hours. You get backstage access, insider information, and best of all—you skip all of the lines! Also included is complimentary breakfast, valet parking, reserved seating at shows and more. A VIP experience is the only way to ensure that you will experience every attraction which is open, regardless of crowds.

You can choose to VIP with a group or for a higher fee, have your own private VIP experience.

The 1-Day, 2-Park Experience is a seven hour tour with priority entrance into a minimum of ten rides and attractions.

The 1-Day, 1-Park Experience is a five hour tour with priority entrance into a minimum of eight major rides and attractions at the park of your choice

Here are some benefits of the VIP experience:

- Priority front-of-the-line access to all rides and attractions including The Amazing Adventures of Spider-Man®, TRANSFORMERS: The Ride-3D and all of The Wizarding World of Harry Potter™ attractions and experiences

- Exclusive behind-the-scenes experiences in the parks (subject to availability)

- Complimentary valet parking (one vehicle, based on availability)

- Reserved seating at shows (excludes live performances during Mardi Gras and Mannheim Steamroller during the holidays)

- Complimentary continental breakfast and lunch

- Universal Express Unlimited™ ride access at participating rides and attractions throughout the rest of the day (during normal park operating hours)

- Exclusive VIP Experiences lanyard and credential

- Universal CityWalk Party Pass™, valid only on date of VIP Experience (during normal CityWalk™ park operating hours)

- Discounts at select Universal Orlando owned and operated merchandise locations in the theme parks and CityWalk™

NOTE: Separate theme park admission is required for VIP Experiences. Admission is not included in the price of any VIP Experience.

Both 1-Day, 1-Park Experiences at Universal Studios Florida™ and 1-Day, 1-Park Experiences to Universal's Islands of Adventure™ will receive one Universal Dining Plan – Quick Service™ meal per person. All 2-Park Non-Private Experiences will receive a chef-catered lunch buffet at the Premium Dining Experience in Café La Bamba, which is not open to the general public. Breakfast is included for all tour types starting at or before 11:00 am.

VIP Breakfast Menu
Available to Private and Non-Private VIP Experience Guests for tours starting at or before 11:00AM

Eggs	Biscuits
Bacon	Gravy
Sausage	Roasted Potatoes
Cherry Danishes	Blueberry Muffins
Apple Danishes	Croissants
Strawberry Yogurt	Assorted Fruits
Milk	Apple Juice
Chocolate Milk	Water
Orange Juice	

VIP Lunch Menu

Signature Dishes

Confisco's Beef Medallions
Grilled beef medallions served with fresh broccoli

Mojo Pork
Cuban-Style pork served with Spanish rice

Monsters Cafe's BBQ Ribs
Monster Cafe's famous BBQ ribs

Seafood

Mytho's Salmon Medallions with Pink Peppercorn Butter Sauce
Seasoned salmon medallions cooked in pink peppercorn butter sauce

Finnegan's Baked Cod
Fresh fillet of cod lightly covered with seasoned bread crumbs baked golden brown

Poultry

Grilled Chicken Marsala
Chicken breast covered in creamy marsala wine sauce with sliced mushrooms
Monsters Cafe's Oven Roasted Chicken
Oven roasted rotisserie chicken

Chicken Tenders
Breaded chicken strips served with wedge potato fries

Garde Manger

Orzo Pasta Salad
Orzo pasta cooked in a tomato base with salt, pepper, and chives

Red Bliss Potato Salad
Classic red potato salad

Pasta Salad
Pasta salad in Italian dressing with red onions, pepperoncini, black olives, mozzarella cheese, and salami

Pasta

Macaroni & Cheese
Elbow macaroni covered in a creamy cheddar cheese sauce

Four Cheese Cavatappi
Cavatappi pasta, tossed in our homemade four cheese chimichurri sauce. Topped with chicken and chorizo.

Gnocchi alla Sorrentina
Gnocchi pasta, tossed in marinara sauce. Topped with basil and fresh Mozzarella cheese.

Salad

Choices of mixed greens and romaine lettuce with a selection of toppings including cucumbers, onions, tomatoes, black olives, green peppers, bacon, and chicken

Dressings: Caesar, Ranch, Blue Cheese, Italian

Tip: Doing a VIP Tour is perfect for guests who want to experience all of the rides. However, they follow a structured plan with a timeline and little

room for variation unless you do a private VIP tour. If you want more flexibility, purchasing Universal Express might be better for your group.

For more information about VIP tours, contact the VIP Call Center at (866) 346-9350.

Touring Plans

The first touring plan is for a one day adventure at Islands of Adventure. This is specifically for those with young children who who want no thrill rides. Just remember, with young kids, you might not be able to experience each and every ride in one day. Pick and choose your favorites on this list. If you still have time, do the rest.

Arriving at the Parks

It takes a while to get to the parks, even if you are staying onsite. For onsite guests, the quickest way to the parks is to take the walking path. Onsite guests should always take advantage of the exclusive benefit, Early Park Admission. Going through security and bag check also takes extra time. Allow extra travel time into your day's plan, at least 30 minutes.

Tip: Bring a change of clothes and wear waterproof shoes such as flip flops for the water rides in Toon Lagoon. You will get soaked!

If you do not have early park admission, arrive at

least 45 minutes prior to the posted park opening time. Once inside the gates, grab a park map, check the listed Character Zones and head straight to Hogsmeade. Turn right after Port of Entry and turn left before Caro-seuss-el and follow the path around. Turn left and head through the Lost Continent to Hogsmeade. Follow this list of attractions.

Kid's Rule Touring Plan for Islands of Adventure-No Thrills

Location	Attraction
Head to Jurassic Park	Pteranodon Flyers. Guests over 56" in height must be accompanied by a guest 36" to 56" in height.
Head to Hogsmeade	
	Ollivanders Wand Chooses the Wizard Show
	Flight of the Hippogriff, minimum height 36"
Snack time	Enjoy a Butterbeer, either original or frozen
	Spell casting with an interactive wand at designated spots
	Frog Choir or Tri-Wizard Spirit Rally performances
Head to Jurassic Park	
	Playtime at Camp Jurassic. Be prepared to spend a considerable amount of time here.
	Jurassic Park Discovery Center. Be prepared to spend a considerable amount of time here.

Location	Attraction
Lunch	Have lunch at Burger Digs or Pizza Predatoria. You may also head back to Hogsmeade to The Three Broomsticks or Mythos, a full service restaurant, in The Lost Continent.
Head to The Lost Continent	
	The Mystic Fountain—an interactive talking fountain—chance to get wet.
	Poseidon's Fury—a walkthrough attraction with special effects
Head to Seuss Landing	
Snack time	Enjoy a cotton candy twice the size of your head from Honk Honkers, ice cream at Hop on Pops Ice cream shop, or a sweet confection from Snooker & Snooker Sweet Candy Cooker
	High in the Sky Seuss Trolley Train
	Caro-Seuss-el
	If I Ran the Zoo Play Area
	Oh' the Stories You'll Hear Show—check showtimes
	The Cat in the Hat
	One Fish Two Fish Red Fish Blue Fish—chance to get wet
Dinner Option 1	Have dinner at Circus McGurus Cafe Stoo-Pendus or Green Eggs and Ham Cafe, open seasonally
Head to Marvel Super Hero Island	
	Storm Force Acceltron

Location	Attraction
	Photos with Spiderman at the Marvel AlterUniverse Store across the street from Cafe4.
	Character Meet and Greets. The character are out very often in this area. If you don't see any, wait 15 or 20 minutes and they will come out.
	Explore the comic book artwork. If you know anything about Marvel characters, you'll recognize many in the artwork exploding off the buildings. Count the heroes and villains you see. The artwork extends into the restaurants and shops.
Dinner Option 2	Have dinner at Cafe4 or Captain America Diner—Cafe4 hosts Marvel Super Hero Character Dinner on select nights—reservations recommended
Head to Toon Lagoon	
	Popeye & Bluto's Bilge-Rat Barges (you will get soaked—that's a fact! While you are wet, Ride Dudley Do-Right's Ripsaw Falls. There is one steep drop and you will get soaked.
	Me Ship The Olive Play Area. A nice way to end the day, and dry off, before heading back to your hotel.

Kids Rule! Touring Plan for Universal Studios-No Thrills

Location	Attraction
Production Central	Despicable Me Minion Mayhem—multi-dimentional ride which makes some guests queasy

Location	Attraction
	Shrek 4-D
Diagon Alley	
Snack time	Florean Fortescue's Ice Cream Parlour
	Gringotts Money Exchange-Goblin Character
	Ollivanders Wand Chooses the Wizard Show
	Spell Casting at designated spell locations
	Tales of Beedle the Bard Puppet Shows—at random times which are usually not listed
	Celestina Warbeck and the Banshees Show—at random times
Lunch option 1	The Leaky Cauldron
The London Waterfront	The Knight Bus—interactive character experience
World Expo	Men in Black Aliens Attack—some spinning. Belonging must be placed in a locker
	Ask for an Immigration Room Tour at Men in Black—only available during slow periods
Lunch Option 2	Lunch at Kidzone Pizza Company
Woody Woodpecker's KidZone	Animal Actor's on Location—check showtimes.
	Barney's Backyard Play Area
	A Day in the Park with Barney—check showtimes
	Curious George Goes to Town Play Area—some wet areas
	The Ball Factory—Inside the Curious George area
	Woody Woodpecker's Nuthouse Coaster—a kiddie roller coaster

Location	Attraction
Snack time	Dippin Dots
	Fievel's Playland play area and water slide
	E.T. Adventure
Dinner	Fast Food Boulevard in the Simpsons area
The Simpson area	Kang & Kodos' Twirl 'n Hurl
Dessert	Lard Lad
	The Simpsons Ride — A multi-dimensional ride which makes some guests queasy.
	Cinematic Spectacular nightly show with fireworks

Tip: While at in the Simpsons area, purchase The Big Pink Donut to take with you have have for breakfast the next day or late night snack.

Teens Touring Plans

Many teens usually have little patience for "baby" rides and want to head straight to the serious roller coasters. Some teens are Harry Potter fanatics (along with their parents) and just want to hang out and cast spells all day. Some teens want to do both. Here are touring plans to accommodate each type.

If you are a big J. K. Rowling fan and only have one day to tour, skip the rest of the parks. There is so much to see in the Diagon Alley area, and you don't want to miss any of it. Diagon Alley is designed as a hidden area as the books describe.

There are no signs indicating that it is there and non-Potter fans might walk right past the London area. However, this area is a giant draw to Muggles of all ages! Even during slow periods, it can get quite crowded very early and stay that way all day. I've created this touring plan by request because it's such an immersive experience. You are truly entering a "wizarding world" and it deserves a dedicated day!

Choose a one-day Park-to-Park ticket and arrive early at Universal Studios Florida. Upon arrival, grab a park map and go directly to Diagon Alley and follow this list of attractions:

Harry Potter Fan One-Day Touring Plan

To take advantage of this plan, you must have a park to park ticket.

Location	Attraction
Hogsmeade	Hagrid's Magical Creatures Motorbike Adventure
	Harry Potter and the Hidden Journey
Diagon Alley	Ride the Hogwarts Express to Diagon Alley
	Ollivanders—After the show, purchase an interactive wand.
	Spell Casting at designated spell locations
Snack time	Florean Fortescue's Ice Cream Parlour
	Gringotts Money Exchange—wizard money exchange to spend in the wizarding world and speak to the goblin clerk
	Browse the shops in Diagon Alley

Location	Attraction
The London Waterfront	Hogwarts Express Train Ride to Hogsmeade
Lunch	The Three Broomsticks
	Cast Spells at designated spell locations
	Flight of the Hippogriff
Snack time	Butterbeer at the Hogs Head Pub
	Watch the Frog Choir or Tri-Wizard Spirit Rally— showtimes vary
	Browse shops in Hogsmeade
	Send a letter or postcard at Owl Post
	Hogwarts Express Train Ride to London
	Harry Potter and the Forbidden Journey
The London Waterfront	The Knight Bus—Interactive Character Meet and Greet
	No. 12 Grimmauld Place—see Kreacher look out of upstairs window
	Look for Easter Eggs (hidden objects) in the shop windows
	Dial MAGIC at the Red Phone Booth
Diagon Alley	Dinner at the Leaky Cauldron
	Knockturn Alley
	Shop at Borgin and Burkes-Knockturn
	Tales of Beedle the Bard and Celestina Warbeck show

Two-Day Harry Potter Touring Plan

To take advantage of this plan, you must have a park to park ticket.

Day	Location	Attraction
Day 1	Diagon Alley	Breakfast at The Leaky Cauldron
		Harry Potter and the Escape from Gringotts
		Ollivanders
		Ollivanders Wand Shop—buy interactive wand
	Snack	Florean Fortescue's Ice Cream Parlour
		Cast spells!
		Gringotts Money Exchange
	London Waterfront	
	Lunch	London Taxi Stand—try a Jacket Potato
		Red Phone booth—dial MAGIC
	Snack	Try some sweet treats purchase at Sugarplums or Weasleys Wizard Wheezes
		Knight Bus
		No. 12 Grimmauld Place—see Kreacher
	Diagon Alley	
	Dinner	The Hopping Pot
	London Waterfront	Hogwarts Express to Hogsmeade

Day	Location	Attraction
	Snack	Butterbeer
		Hogwarts Nightly Lights Show
Day 2	Hogsmeade	
		Hagrid's Magical Creatures Motorbike Adventure
	Breakfast	The Three Broomsticks
		Harry Potter and the Forbidden Journey
		Cast spells!
		Send a post card at Owl Post
	Snack	Pumpkin juice on tap at Hogs Head Pub
		Flight of the Hippogriff
	Lunch	The Three Broomsticks or for a change, go to Mythos in The Lost Continent
		Browse the shops of Hogsmeade. Take note when the Owl Clock tower hoots the hour!
		Hogwarts Express to London
	Diagon Alley	Shutterbuttons Photo Shoot
		Visit Owl Post to purchase special packaging shipped anywhere in the continental United States
	Snack	Try Butterbeer fudge at Sugarplums
		Take a break from the heat in Knockturn Alley.
		Look for Easter Eggs in Knockturn Alley.

Day	Location	Attraction
	Dinner	Leaky Cauldron—if you haven't already, try Butterbeer Potted Cream

Teens Rule! All Thrills One-Day Touring Plan for Islands of Adventure

Location	Attraction
Hogsmeade	Hagrid's Magical Creatures Motorbike Adventure
Marvel Super Hero Island	The Incredible Hulk Coaster
Skull Island	Skull Island-Reign of Kong
Hogsmeade	Harry Potter and the Forbidden Journey
Lunch	The Three Broomsticks
	Flight of the Hippogriff
Snack	Brookie from Pizza Predatoria
Jurassic Park	Jurassic Park River Adventure—you may get wet
Marvel Super Hero Island	The Amazing Adventure of Spider-Man
	Doctor Doom's Fearfall
Dinner	Cafe4
Toon Lagoon	Popeye & Bluto's Bilge Rat Barges—you will get soaked
	Dudley Do-Right's Ripsaw Falls—you will get soaked

Teens Rule! All Thrills Touring Plan for Universal Studios

Location	Attractions
Production Central	Hollywood Rip Ride Rockit Coaster
	Despicable Me Minion Mayhem
New York	Race Through New York Starring Jimmy Fallon
Lunch	Monsters Cafe, Louie's Italian Restaurant, Finnegans
	Revenge of the Mummy
Production Central	Transformers: The Ride 3D
San Francisco	Fast & Furious—Supercharged
Diagon Alley	Harry Potter and the Escape from Gringotts
	Fear Factor Live—check showtimes
World Expo	Men in Black—Aliens Attack
Springfield	
Dinner	Fast Food Boulevard
	The Simpsons Ride

15 STRATEGIC SOUVENIR SHOPPING

Shopping for souvenirs can be a tricky business, especially if you're vacationing on a budget. Putting cost aside, the time it takes to shop should be planned out.

The best time to arrive at the themeparks is prior to opening time or take advantage of Early Park Admission for onsite hotel guests. This is when there are fewer guests and lines for attractions are shorter. As far as shopping goes, the best strategy is to avoid shopping until later in the day. Every attraction exits through a gift shop themed to that ride. Fight the impulse to stop and shop, but take mental notes and wait to make purchases after lunch.

There is an exception to this rule. If you are a Harry Potter fan, purchase an interactive wand as soon as you arrive! Whether you buy at the end of the Ollivanders experience or from a street vendor, these wands are a big part of the Diagon Alley experience and can be used in Hogsmeade as well. You will get a themed map with locations of spell spots.

In the case of The Wizarding World of Harry Potter, perusing the whimsical shops is part of touring these areas. Depending on your budget, make a plan of where you want to shop and what to do with your purchases.

Package Delivery

If you plan to make lots of purchases, you don't have to carry them around all day. Besides renting an all day locker, there are other options. At Owl Post in Diagon Alley, your purchasing can be prepared for shipment in special packaging and shipped anywhere in the United States.

Another option for purchases is to have them held for you at Guest Services. Shop attendants will give you instructions for the timing of pickup of your packages before the park's closing time. Don't forget to pickup before you leave!

Onsite guests may have their purchases sent to their hotel rooms. However, your purchases may not be available until the next day so don't do this on the last night of your stay.

Tip: You can shop before you get there! Visit UniversalOrlando.com to purchase items from the Wizarding World, Minions, Marvel, etc. Make your purchases in advance so you don't waste valuable ride time in shops. You can also shop online auction sites like ebay.com to purchase interactive wands.

Themed Shops

As you exit each attraction, you enter a shop appropriately themed to the attraction. In each area of the park, there are very specific items to be found. Accordingly, you probably won't find Dr. Doom t-shirts in Springfield.

Allow time in your park touring schedule and make notes in your smartphone of where you saw certain items that you want. Refer to these notes before exiting the park for the last time.

Discounts

There are a couple of ways to save a little when shopping at the theme parks. The best way is to get discounts. There are several ways to get discounts. Here are the best ways:

Join AAA. Not only is AAA a great travelers' resource offering trip mapping, free guide books, and roadside service, but also allows members to get discounts on hotels, restaurants and merchandise. There is usually a minimum purchase at each shop.

Use your discount from onsite and official offsite hotels. These hotels give discount cards to guests which can be used for restaurants and retail stores. If you purchased multiple day tickets, you will receive a $150 coupon book—receive it in the mail or pick up on arrival.

Tip: Preferred and Premier Passholders receive discounts on merchandise.

Tip: If you won't use it, don't buy it. This is a good rule to follow when shopping for souvenirs. Buy items that you will use often. If you will use a tumbler, mug, key chain or wear a t-shirt often, then you won't have "buyers remorse."

Tip: Collect Penny Keepsakes! Collecting Penny Keepsakes can be a fun activity with cool souvenirs to keep. Penny Keepsakes are created from machines at various locations around the parks. You place a penny in the slot and pay about $1.00, crank the handle and your penny will "magically" be transformed into a pressed keepsake. Each machine presses different images which correspond to that area of the park. It is a fun activity to look for the machines in each area of the parks, collect pressed pennies from each machine and trade them with friends and family.

Shopping by Location

Here is a list of shops by location in the theme

parks and CityWalk.

Shops at Universal Studios

Hollywood Shops
> Cyber Image—Near Horror Make-Up Show
> Brown Derby Hat Shop
> Williams of Hollywood—Sells props and more
> from closed attractions and previous events.

Production Central Shops
> Universal Studios Store
> Super Silly Stuff—Despicable Me
> Hello Kitty
> Betty Boop Store
> Supply Vault—Transformers
> Studio Sweets
> Shrek's Ye Olde Souvenir Shoppe

New York Shops
> The Film Vault
> Rosie's Irish Shop
> Sahara Traders
> Park Plaza Holiday Shop
> Amazing Pictures

San Francisco Shops
> Custom Gear—Fast & Furious
> San Francisco Candy Factory

The London Waterfront
> London Taxi Stand

Diagon Alley Shops
  Gringotts Money Exchange
  Weasley Wizard Wheezes
  Sugarplums Sweet Shop
  Borgin and Burkes—Knockturn Alley
  Ollivanders
  Shutterbuttons
  Globus Mundi
  Wiseacre's Wizarding Equipment
  Scribbulus
  Wands by Gregorovitch

World Expo Shops
  MIB Gear

Woody Woodpecker's KidZone Shops
  E.T.'s Toy Closet
  The Barney Shop
  SpongeBob StorePants

Shops at Islands of Adventure

Port of Entry Shops
  Port of Entry Christmas Shop
  Islands of Adventure Trading Company
  Port Provisions
  Ocean Trader
  Island Market Export Candy Shoppe

Seuss Landing Shops
  Mulberry Street Store
  All the Books You Can Read

Cats, Hats and Things
Snookers & Snookers Sweet Candy Cookers

The Lost Continent Shops
Mythical Metals
Star Souls
Treasures of Poseidon
Historic Families—Heraldy
Shop of Wonders

Hogsmeade Shops
Honeydukes
Ollivanders
Dervish and Banges
Filch's Emporium of Confiscated Goods
Owl Post

Jurassic Park Shops
Dinostore
Jurassic Outfitters

Toon Lagoon Shops
Betty Boop Store
Toon Extra
Gasoline Alley
Wossamotta-U

Marvel Super Hero Island Shops
Comic Book Store
Spider-Man Store
Marvel Alterniverse Store

Universal CityWalk Shopping
    Hart & Huntington Tattoo Company
    Fossil
    P!Q
    Fresh Produce
    Quiet Flight Surf Shop
    Rock Shop—Hard Rock Cafe
    Universal Studios Store
    The Island Clothing Co.

16 DISABILITIES AND SPECIAL NEEDS

If someone in your party has special needs, one of your first stops when you arrive at Universal Studios or Islands of Adventure is to visit Guest Services inside the parks and near the front entrances.

The Attraction Assistance Pass is issued upon request to guests whose disability makes them unable to wait in lines for attractions. You will be asked to explain your disability. Universal has adopted Disney's policy and no longer issues this pass to guests who cannot stand in long lines because of physical disabilities. These guests are told to rent a wheelchair.

If you are issued this pass, you will receive a "come-back time" for most attractions to avoid the regular lines. For more information about services offered or ride details, download the Guide for Riders Safety. Visit this site for more information on rider safety.

Tip: If you pay for your rented ECV with a credit card instead of cash, you can return it at either park!

Wheelchairs, ECV's and Attractions

If you require a wheelchair or Electric Conveyance Vehicle (motorized scooter, referred to as ECV), limited quantities are available for daily rental. You can make a reservation in advance for a wheelchair, ECV or stroller. Any unreserved items are rented on a first come, first served basis. Wheelchair Rental facilities are located in the Parking and Transportation Center (known as "the Hub") and at rental counters inside both theme park entrances. Wheelchair and ECV rentals require a deposit (usually $50).

Tip: Always make a reservation for an ECV as the parks run out of them on a regular basis! Call Guest Services to reserve at (407) 224-4233.

Certain attractions are capable of allowing guests to remain in their standard manual wheelchair throughout:

ISLANDS OF ADVENTURE

Camp Jurassic®
Caro-Seuss-el
The Hogwarts Express – HogsmeadeTM Station
If I Ran the Zoo

Jurassic Park Discovery Center®
Me Ship, The Olive®
One Fish, Two Fish, Red Fish, Blue Fish
Poseidon's Fury®
The Cat in the Hat

UNIVERSAL STUDIOS®

A Day in the Park with BarneyTM
Animal Actors On Location!®
Curious George Goes to Town
Despicable Me Minion Mayhem®
E .T . Adventure®
Fear Factor Live
Fievel's Playland®
The Hogwarts Express – King's Cross Station
MEN IN BLACKTM Alien Attack • Shrek 4-D
Universal Orlando's Horror Make-Up Show

Due to the unique nature of the vehicles at several attractions, specific vehicles have been designed to easily accommodate guests transferring from their wheelchair. These attractions include:

ISLANDS OF ADVENTURE

Dudley Do-Right's Ripsaw Falls®
Flight of the Hippogriff
Jurassic Park River Adventure®
Popeye & Bluto's Bilge-Rat Barges®
Storm Force Accelatron®

UNIVERSAL STUDIOS®

Despicable Me Minion Mayhem®
Harry Potter and the Escape from Gringotts
Kang & Kodos' Twirl 'n' Hurl
MEN IN BLACK Alien Attack
Woody Woodpecker's Nuthouse Coaster®

With the exception of the Hogwarts Express, ECV's and motorized wheelchairs are not allowed on any of the ride vehicles or in attraction queues at Universal Orlando. Guests may transfer from their ECV or motorized wheelchair into a manual wheelchair which is provided at each location.

Guests using Oxygen Tanks/Devices

Due to the dramatic movement of the ride vehicles and certain special effects at Universal Orlando, oxygen tanks are only permitted at the following locations:

ISLANDS OF ADVENTURE

Camp Jurassic® (except Pteranodon Flyers®)
The Eighth Voyage of Sindbad®
The Hogwarts Express – Hogsmeade Station
Toon Amphitheater

UNIVERSAL STUDIOS®

A Day in the Park with Barney®
Animal Actors On Location!®

Curious George Goes to Town
Despicable Me Minion Mayhem® (stationary seating only)
Fear Factor Live
Fievel's Playland® (except water slide)
The Hogwarts Express – King's Cross Station
Shrek 4-D (stationary seating only)
Universal Orlando's Horror Make-Up Show

Guests with Vision Disabilities

Park guests with vision disabilities can get park guide information, restaurant menus, and attraction scripts, available in large font and embossed in Braille at the Guest Services lobbies at Universal Studios and Islands of Adventure.

For guests with a white cane, many attractions provide a basket or receptacle in which to place the cane in the ride vehicle, but the cane may need to be collapsed on some attractions. On attractions where the cane may become lost due to ride forces and present a potential hazard to other guests, the Attraction Attendant will hold the white cane for the guest once the guest is seated and return it as soon as the attraction vehicle is stopped in the unload area.

White canes will be held by an attendant at the following attractions:

ISLANDS OF ADVENTURE

Caro-Seuss-el
Doctor Doom's Fearfall®
Flight of the Hippogriff
Harry Potter and the Forbidden Journey
The Incredible Hulk Coaster® • Pteranodon
Flyers®

UNIVERSAL STUDIOS®

E .T . Adventure®
Fievel's Playland® water slide
Harry Potter and the Escape from Gringotts
Hollywood Rip Ride Rockit®
MEN IN BLACK Aliens Attack
Revenge of the Mummy®
Woody Woodpecker's Nuthouse Coaster®

Service Animals

Service animals are welcome in all restaurants and merchandise locations, attraction queues and most other locations throughout Universal Orlando. There are specific entry/boarding requirements for each attraction to assist the owner in making an informed decision about their animal's safe admission. Refer to the Riders Guide for each attraction's details. If you choose to ride without your service animal, portable kennels are available. Speak to the Attraction Attendant at any of the rides or shows for further assistance.

Service animals have specific places in the parks to be "walked." A small patch of grass is provided "behind the scenes" for your animal's private business. Walking areas are available for your service animal at the following locations:

ISLANDS OF ADVENTURE

Marvel Super Hero Island® between The Amazing Adventures of Spider-Man® and Doctor Doom's Fearfall®

Jurassic Park® behind Pizza Predattoria®

Seuss LandingTM behind One Fish, Two Fish, Red Fish, Blue Fish

UNIVERSAL STUDIOS®

In Central Park across from Cafe La Bamba
World Expo between MEN IN BLACK Alien Attack and Fear Factor Live

Guests with Prostheses

Guests must remove all prosthetic limbs before riding the following attractions to prevent hazards or loss due to ride forces:

ISLANDS OF ADVENTURE
Pteranodon Flyers®
UNIVERSAL STUDIOS®
Hollywood Rip Ride Rockit®

Guests must properly secure or remove all prosthetic limbs before riding the following attractions to prevent hazards or loss due to ride forces:

ISLANDS OF ADVENTURE
Doctor Doom's Fearfall®
Dudley Do-Right's Ripsaw Falls®
Flight of the Hippogriff
Harry Potter and the Forbidden Journey
The Incredible Hulk Coaster®
Jurassic Park River Adventure
UNIVERSAL STUDIOS®
Harry Potter and the Escape from Gringotts
Revenge of the Mummy®
Woody Woodpecker's Nuthouse Coaster®

Casts or Braces

Guests with casts or braces will be restricted from riding The Incredible Hulk Coaster, where the cast or brace may present a hazard to the guest or others. Consult with the attraction attendants or Guest Services for more information.

Special Needs Amenities at Onsite Hotels

At onsite resorts, there are features for guests with disabilities. Chair lifts have been installed at all pools and spas. All entrances to individual guest rooms include the room number in Braille. Hearing Impaired Kits (that include a TDD relay service) are available from Star Service and may be used in any guest room.

In guest rooms, the following modifications have been made:

- Entry doors are 36" wide
- Doors with peepholes at 3'6" from the floor
- Closets with rods at 48" high
- Toilets with hand bar
- Bathroom choices
- Roll-in shower stall with adjustable shower head or combination shower/tub with adjustable shower head, tub seat, and hand bar
- Closed-caption television
- Smoke detector with light

17 UNIVERSAL'S VOLCANO BAY

Traveling to Florida's hot and humid tropical climate creates a need to cool off. A water park visit is the best way to cool off and have fun! Just in time for your vacation, Universal Orlando has opened Volcano Bay, a new water park! The centerpiece of the park is a towering volcano which "erupts" from time to time. It is an immersive experience, with slides, waterfalls, a wave pool, and a water coaster.

Volcano Bay is way ahead of other parks as far as technology. Volcano Bay has instituted a virtual line system called TapuTapu, a wearable technology (worn on the wrist). You can use the Universal smartphone App to create an account and link a credit card so that you can go cashless all day!

Volcano Bay is located next to Cabana Bay Beach Resort with a special entrance for guests of that resort.

Before you Go

Since most families will travel to Universal Orlando in the summer when crowds are at their peak, here are a few tips to know before you go to Volcano Bay.

Purchase Tickets Online

You'll save valuable time and money by purchasing your Volcano Bay tickets online before you go. The ticket window lines can be quite long, especially during the summer when most families choose to visit. Tickets can be purchase separately as part of a 3-Park package or an add-on to annual passes.

Stay Onsite at Cabana Bay Beach Resort

Guests of Cabana Bay Beach Resort and all of the onsite hotels are allowed admission to Volcano Bay one hour prior to opening time. This is very important because the park often reaches capacity early in the day in the summer and the crowds make visiting the attractions very difficult. Even with Tapu Tapu, the virtual wait time can be hours long. Cabana Bay Beach Resort is great because guests can walk to the entrance and even leave for a lunchbreak.

Head to the Back of the Park

The lockers at the entrance of the park are

usually quite crowded. What many don't know is that there is another set of lockers on the other side of the volcano. Head to the back of the park, get you locker and set up a base camp for the day.

Rent a Space for the Day

If you're planning your trip during a busy time or you would like to elevate your Volcano Bay experience, renting a space for the day is a great idea. If you would like to do this, make reservations! There are a limited number and they book up quickly! The pricing for these seating options vary depending on the time of year and expected crowds.

Premium Seating includes a pair of padded lounge chairs with a retractable shade canopy. There is a lock box for valuables and you get wait service to bring you food and drinks all day. Prices for Premium seating begin at $49.99 per day.

Single Cabana Units hold up to 6 people. You have a choice of upper level cabanas with great views, ground level cabanas for convenience and accessibility, or standalone cabanas that offer a bit more privacy. Prices for Single Cabana Units begin at $199.99 per day.

Family Suite Cabanas hold up to 16 people. Relax with your group in a large, private stand-alone cabana. Prices start at $599.99 per day.

TapuTapu Virtual Lines

TapuTapu is a waterproof device worn on the wrist, exclusive to Volcano Bay. TapuTapu uses Virtual Line technology and also triggers multiple interactive surprises throughout the park. This innovative technology is the first of its kind and, while users have experienced a few issues in the beginning, Universal is working hard to fix any technical issues.

Here are Universal Orlando's instructions on how to use TapuTapu:

• Receive your TapuTapu wearable device as you enter the park. Every guest will receive TapuTapu for the day.

• Look for totems marked with the Volcano Bay logo at the entrance to each attraction. Upon touching your TapuTapu to the totems, you'll be able to hold your place in line with a Virtual Line. While you wait you can explore the park, float in one of two rivers or grab a bite to eat. Your TapuTapu will alert you when it's time to ride.

• You'll also be able to unlock interactive surprises throughout the park. Control streams of water spurting from whales in Tot Tiki Reef. Shoot water cannons at other guests snaking down Kopiko Wai Winding River. Or illuminate images in the volcano's hidden caves.

• Return your TapuTapu as you exit the park.

The Attractions at Volcano Bay

Volcano Bay is made up of four different sections: The Volcano, Wave Village, River Village and Rainforest Village.

The Volcano

The centerpiece of the park is Krakatau™ (named after one of the world's most famous volcanos in islands of Indonesia), the mighty Fire and Water Volcano. Towering 200 feet above the tropical landscape, Krakatau streams waterfalls during the day and fiery lava effects at night.

Krakatau™ Aqua Coaster

A state of the art water coaster resides inside Krakatau. Four-person canoes slide upward through the mists and into dark twists and turns within the volcano before emerging with a plunge through a shimmering waterfall.

Ko'okiri Body Plunge

The Ko'okiri Body Plunge features a 70-degree fall through a drop door and 125 feet of screaming, white-knuckle fun, this dizzying descent ends with a watery tribute from Vol himself.

Kala & Tai Nui Serpentine Body Slides

Twin trap doors simultaneously drop two guests down clear, intertwining tubes before sending them splashing into the turquoise waters below.

Punga Racers

A favorite among children of all ages, Punga

Racers send single riders on their manta ray mats sliding down four lanes through underwater sea caves.

Wave Village

This peaceful escape overlooks the sparkling waters of Waturi Beach at the base of the volcano.

Waturi Beach

Swim, splash and relax in the sparkling waters and warm waves of this sparkling lagoon at the foot of Krakatau.

River Village

The scenic River Village has fun for people of all ages, including the very youngest child or child at heart.

Honu of the Honu ika Moana

Just like the ancient Waturi people who rode the ocean waves on friendly sea turtles and whales, guests can enjoy these two twisting, turning, multi-person slides. Honu sweeps up two massive walls, while Ika Moana sprays water on riders from the center of the raft.

Tot Tiki Reef

Little tots can play among splashy slides, a tot-sized water volcano and a family of friendly tikis with spraying fountains. Plus, adorable whales spray and sing as kids raise and lower their hands.

Runamukka Reef

Runamukka Reef™ is a play place for young children with its bubbling geysers, water guns, slides and dump cups. Shaded by fanciful bamboo sea creatures and waving seaweed.

Kopiko Wai Winding River

Take a slow ride on the Kopiko Wai Winding River. Sprays of water surprise along the way, and beneath the lava rocks, Stargazer's Cavern reveals the magical night sky above.

Rainforest Village

Rainforest Village stretches along the shores of an action-packed river and features the perfect mix of relaxation and exhilaration.

Ohyah + Ohno Drop Slides

Test your mettle and get into the Waturi spirit. Ascend cliff side and plummet down the twisting waters of Ohyah before dropping out four feet above the pool below. To achieve even greater bragging rights, brave the rope bridge and plunge down Ohno, a serpentine adventure that ends six feet above the pool below.

Maku Puihi Round Raft Rides

Ready for the high adventure of the Maku Puihi lava tubes? This six-person racing rafting adventure is a favorite of families who want more than a lazy river. Choose one of two paths or try them bot. Puihi careens through a dark, winding tunnel before the stomach-flipping thrill of zero gravity hang time. Maku slides you through a deep volcanic gorge before spinning wildly around bowl-like formations.

TeAwa The Fearless River

TeAwa The Fearless River is a thrilling whitewater ride. Race along a roaring, watery onslaught of churning rapids and choppy waves hanging tight to your inner tube.

Taniwha Tubes

Taniwha Tubes consists of four twisting water slides. Riders can try all four twisting tracks.

Dining at Volcano Bay

A lot a planning and development has gone into the dining options at Volcano Bay. The dining options have actually been narrowed down from when the park opened and best options are even better. Flavors of the islands are definitely present as well as all of the kids favorites. Most eateries are quick service for convenience and those who have reserved seating may order food and drinks to be delivered to them.

Whakawaiwai Eats

Waves of Flavors are available here including Island BBQ Chicken Pizza, Tropical Baby Greens salad, Hawaiian Pizza and a crowd favorite, Jerk Shrimp Mac and Cheese.

The Feasting Frog

Patio seating surrounds this fun structure shaped like a tropical frog. Here you'll find a small menu of drinks and snacks like the Poke Poke Bowl, Taco Sampler, or Plantain Chips & Guacamole.

Bambu

A cool, shaded hideaway made of stalks of bamboo offers a great menu of burgers, salads including vegan options.

Kohola Reef Restaurant & Social Club

This open air cafe across from the wave pool and at the base of the volcano delights with fresh island favorites including a variety of chicken dishes, burgers, and pizzas as well as a grab and go variety of items including sushi rolls, veggie wraps and salads. Try the Mango BBQ Pulled Pork Sandwich or crunchy Coconut Crusted Fried Chicken.

18 FUTURE PLANS

Universal Orlando is continuing its investment in the future. With a commitment to a new ride or attraction each year, the future looks bright at Universal! The resort's complex is growing by leaps and bounds with the announcement of two new hotels in addition to Universal's Aventura Hotel which opened in 2018. With the addition of these three new hotels and the recent opening of a Volcano Bay, this dazzling family entertainment complex will soon have eight onsite hotels in addition to three theme parks! Universal has also purchased a large tract of land nearby and speculation is rampant as to what will reside there in the future!

As for changes in the theme parks, The Eighth Voyage of Sindbad stunt show in the Lost Continent of Islands of Adventure closed in September of 2018. No announcements have been made as to what will take its place but there are construction walls surrounding it.

The ultimate in good news is the opening of a new Harry Potter themed roller coaster in Islands of Adventure! Hagrid's Magical Creatures Motorbike Adventure combines the theme of the lovable Hagrid and connects the parks with the Fantastic Beasts and Where to Find Them films. The ride opens on June 13, 2019.

The annual Celebration of Harry Potter which is usually held in late January was cancelled this year. When the new ride opens, I predict a special celebration!

At CityWalk, Emeril's has closed it doors and construction walls surround the building. No new business has been announced. To fill a lack of breakfast all day long restaurants, Voodoo Doughnut has opened and is hugely popular. It is the most recent addition to CityWalk and is greatly popular for its madcap creations such as Grape Ape and Maple Bacon Bar. These doughnuts are popular at any time of day! If you have some free time while here, CineMark has taken over management of the movie theater at CityWalk.

ABOUT THE AUTHOR

Mary deSilva is a married, mother of two from Louisiana. She is an author, artist, teacher, foodie and avid traveler. From an early age, she has loved theme parks. While she has visited almost every major city in the United States, Hawaii and Mexico, Orlando holds a special place in her heart.

Check out Mary's YouTube channel: CajunDIYDiva
Instagram: @maryfdesilva
Facebook: @marydesilvaauthor
Twitter: @UOMagicTips

Made in the USA
Middletown, DE
01 April 2019